gift

BEYOND BELIEF

ELAINE PAGELS

BEYOND BELIEF

THE SECRET GOSPEL OF THOMAS

RANDOM HOUSE / NEW YORK

Grateful acknowledgment is made to HarperCollins Publishers, Inc.,
for permission to quote from *Meetings with the Archangel*, by Stephen Mitchell.
Copyright © 1998 by Stephen Mitchell. Reprinted by permission
of HarperCollins Publishers, Inc.

Library of Congress Cataloging-in-Publication Data
Pagels, Elaine H.
Beyond belief : the secret Gospel of Thomas / Elaine Pagels
p. cm.
Includes bibliographical references (p.).
ISBN 0-375-50156-8
1. Gospel of Thomas (Coptic Gospel)—Criticism, interpretation, etc.
2. Bible. N.T. John—Criticism, interpretation, etc.
3. Christianity—Essence, genius, nature.-I. Title.
BS2860.T52 P34   2003   229'.8—dc21   2002036840

Random House website address: www.atrandom.com
Printed in the United States of America on acid-free paper
897

Book design by J. K. Lambert

FOR KENT

with love

There is an invisible world out there, and we are living in it.

BILL VIOLA, VIDEO ARTIST

CONTENTS

BEYOND BELIEF

†o†o†o†

FROM THE FEAST OF AGAPE
TO THE NICENE CREED

On a bright Sunday morning in February, shivering in a T-shirt and running shorts, I stepped into the vaulted stone vestibule of the Church of the Heavenly Rest in New York to catch my breath and warm up. Since I had not been in church for a long time, I was startled by my response to the worship in progress—the soaring harmonies of the choir singing with the congregation; and the priest, a woman in bright gold and white vestments, proclaiming the prayers in a clear, resonant voice. As I stood watching, a thought came to me: Here is a family that knows how to face death.

That morning I had gone for an early morning run while my husband and two-and-a-half-year-old son were still sleeping. The previous night I had been sleepless with fear and worry.

Two days before, a team of doctors at Babies Hospital, Columbia Presbyterian Medical Center, had performed a routine checkup on our son, Mark, a year and six months after his successful open-heart surgery. The physicians were shocked to find evidence of a rare lung disease. Disbelieving the results, they tested further for six hours before they finally called us in to say that Mark had pulmonary hypertension, an invariably fatal disease, they told us. How much time? I asked. "We don't know; a few months, a few years."

The following day, a team of doctors urged us to authorize a lung biopsy, a painful and invasive procedure. How could this help? It couldn't, they explained; but the procedure would let them see how far the disease had progressed. Mark was already exhausted by the previous day's ordeal. Holding him, I felt that if more masked strangers poked needles into him in an operating room, he might lose heart—literally—and die. We refused the biopsy, gathered Mark's blanket, clothes, and Peter Rabbit, and carried him home.

Standing in the back of that church, I recognized, uncomfortably, that I needed to be there. Here was a place to weep without imposing tears upon a child; and here was a heterogeneous community that had gathered to sing, to celebrate, to acknowledge common needs, and to deal with what we cannot control or imagine. Yet the celebration in progress spoke of hope; perhaps that is what made the presence of death bearable. Before that time, I could only ward off what I had heard and felt the day before.

I returned often to that church, not looking for faith but because, in the presence of that worship and the people gathered there—and in a smaller group that met on weekdays in the church basement for mutual encouragement—my defenses fell away, exposing storms of grief and hope. In that church I gathered new energy, and resolved, over and over, to face whatever awaited us as constructively as possible for Mark, and for the rest of us.

When people would say to me, "Your faith must be of great help to you," I would wonder, What do they mean? What is faith? Certainly not simple assent to the set of beliefs that worshipers in that church recited every week ("We believe in one God, the Father, the Almighty, maker of heaven and earth . . .")— traditional statements that sounded strange to me, like barely intelligible signals from the surface, heard at the bottom of the sea. Such statements seemed to me then to have little to do with whatever transactions we were making with one another, with ourselves, and—so it was said—with invisible beings. I was acutely aware that we met there driven by need and desire; yet sometimes I dared hope that such communion has the potential to transform us.

I am a historian of religion, and so, as I visited that church, I wondered when and how being a Christian became virtually synonymous with accepting a certain set of beliefs. From historical reading, I knew that Christianity had survived brutal persecution and flourished for generations—even centuries— *before* Christians formulated what they believed into creeds. The origins of this transition from scattered groups to a unified community have left few traces. Although the apostle Paul, about twenty years after Jesus' death, stated "the gospel," which, he says, "I too received" ("that Christ died for our sins according to the Scriptures; that he was buried, and that he was raised on the third day"),[1] it may have been more than a hundred years later that some Christians, perhaps in Rome, attempted to consolidate their group against the demands of a fellow Christian named Marcion, whom they regarded as a false teacher, by introducing formal statements of belief into worship.[2] But only in the *fourth* century, after the Roman emperor Constantine himself converted to the new faith—or at least decriminalized it—did Christian bishops, at the emperor's command, convene in the city of Nicaea, on the Turkish coast, to agree upon a common statement of beliefs—the so-called Nicene Creed, which defines the faith for many Christians to this day.

Yet I know from my own encounters with people in that church, both upstairs and down, believers, agnostics, and seekers—as well as people who don't belong to any church—that what matters in religious experience involves much more than what we believe (or what we do not believe). What *is* Christianity, and what is religion, I wondered, and why do so many of us still find it compelling, whether or not we belong to a church, and despite difficulties we may have with particular beliefs or practices? What is it about Christian tradition that we love—and what is it that we *cannot* love?

From the beginning, what attracted outsiders who walked into a gathering of Christians, as I did on that February morning, was the presence of a group joined by spiritual power into an extended family. Many must have come as I had, in distress; and some came without money. In Rome, the sick who frequented the temples of Asclepius, the Greek god of healing, expected to pay when they consulted his priests about herbs, exercise, baths, and medicine. These priests also arranged for visitors to spend nights sleeping in the temple precincts, where the god was said to visit his suppliants in dreams. Similarly, those who sought to enter into the mysteries of the Egyptian goddess Isis, seeking her protection and blessings in this life, and eternal life beyond the grave, were charged considerable initiation fees and spent more to buy the ritual clothing, offerings, and equipment.

Irenaeus, the leader of an important Christian group in provincial Gaul in the second century, wrote that many newcomers came to Christian meeting places hoping for miracles, and some found them: "We heal the sick by laying hands on them, and drive out demons," the destructive energies that cause mental instability and emotional anguish. Christians took no money, yet Irenaeus acknowledged no limits to what the spirit could do: "We even raise the dead, many of whom are still alive among us, and completely healthy."[3]

Even without a miracle, those in need could find immediate practical help almost anywhere in the empire, whose great cities—Alexandria in Egypt, Antioch, Carthage, and Rome itself— were then, as now, crowded with people from throughout the known world. Inhabitants of the vast shantytowns that surrounded these cities often tried to survive by begging, prostitution, and stealing. Yet Tertullian, a Christian spokesman of the second century, writes that, unlike members of other clubs and societies that collected dues and fees to pay for feasts, members of the Christian "family" contributed money voluntarily to a common fund to support orphans abandoned in the streets and garbage dumps. Christian groups also brought food, medicines, and companionship to prisoners forced to work in mines, banished to prison islands, or held in jail. Some Christians even bought coffins and dug graves to bury the poor and criminals, whose corpses otherwise would lie unburied beyond the city walls. Like Irenaeus, the African convert Tertullian emphasizes that among Christians

> there is no buying and selling of any kind in what belongs to God. On a certain day, each one, if he likes, puts in a small gift, but only if he wants to do so, and only if he be able, for there is no compulsion; everything is voluntary.[4]

Such generosity, which ordinarily could be expected only from one's own family, attracted crowds of newcomers to Christian groups, despite the risks. The sociologist Rodney Stark notes that, shortly before Irenaeus wrote, a plague had ravaged cities and towns throughout the Roman empire, from Asia Minor though Italy and Gaul.[5] The usual response to someone suffering from inflamed skin and pustules, whether a family member or not, was to run, since nearly everyone infected died in agony. Some epidemiologists estimate that the plague killed a third to a half of the imperial population. Doctors could not, of course, treat the disease, and they too fled the deadly virus. Galen, the most famous physician of his age, who attended the family of Emperor Marcus Aurelius, survived what people later called Galen's plague by escaping to a country estate until it was over.

But some Christians were convinced that God's power was with them to heal or alleviate suffering. They shocked their pagan neighbors by staying to care for the sick and dying, believing that, if they themselves should die, they had the power to overcome death. Even Galen was impressed:

> [For] the people called Christians . . . contempt of death is obvious to us every day, and also their self-control in

sexual matters. . . . They also include people who, in self-discipline . . . in matters of food and drink, and in their keen pursuit of justice, have attained a level not inferior to that of genuine philosophers.[6]

Why did Christians act in such extraordinary ways? They would say that their strength came from their encounter with divine power—but it was a power wholly unlike that of the gods whose temples crowded the city streets, and whose images adorned the theaters and public baths. Jupiter and Diana, Isis and Mithras, required their worshipers to offer devotion, pouring out wine, making sacrifices, and contributing money to the priests at their temples. Such gods were understood to act, like human beings, out of self-interest. But Jews and Christians believed that their God, who created humankind, actually *loved* the human race, and evoked love in return. Jesus succinctly summarized Jewish teaching when he said, "You shall love the Lord your God with all your heart, mind, and soul; and you shall love your neighbor as yourself."[7] What God requires is that human beings love one another and offer help—even, or especially, to the neediest.

Such convictions became the practical basis of a radical new social structure. Rodney Stark suggests that we read the following passage from Matthew's gospel "as if for the very first time," in order to feel the power of this new morality as Jesus' early followers and their pagan neighbors must have felt it:[8]

For I was hungry and you gave me food, I was thirsty and you gave me drink. I was a stranger and you welcomed me, I was naked and you clothed me, I was sick and you

visited me, I was in prison and you came to me. . . . Truly,
I say to you, as you did it to one of the least of these my
brethren, you did it to me.[9]

These precepts could hardly have been universally practiced,
yet Tertullian says that members of what he calls the "peculiar
Christian society" practiced them often enough to attract public
notice: "What marks us in the eyes of our enemies is our practice of lovingkindness: 'Only look,' they say, 'look how they love
one another!' "[10]

Tertullian also says that outsiders ridiculed Christians "because we call each other brother and sister." Yet when he writes
his *Defence of the Christians,* he adds that members of "God's
family" also believed that the human family as a whole is inter-
related. Thus, he says, "we are *your* brothers and sisters as well,
by the law of our common mother, nature," although, he con-
cedes,

> perhaps it is more appropriate to call *brother* and *sister*
> those who have come to know God as their father, and
> who, from the same womb of a common ignorance, have
> agonized into the clear light of truth.[11]

The agonizing birth process he refers to is *baptism,* for to join
God's family one had to die—symbolically—and become a new
person. The apostle Paul had said that whoever is plunged into
the baptismal waters and submerged, as in the waters of death,
dies to his or her former self.[12] For many Christians this was a
wrenching event that severed all familiar bonds, including, of

course, those with the families of their birth. Tertullian describes how non-Christian families rejected those who joined this illicit sect:

> The husband . . . casts the wife out of his house; the father . . . disinherits the son; the master commands the slave to depart from his presence: it is a huge offence for anyone to be reformed by this hated name [Christian].[13]

Why a "huge offence"? Because in the eyes of their relatives, converts were joining a cult of criminals—a choice that could be suicidal for the convert, and disastrous for the family left behind. The Roman senator Tacitus, who despised Christians for their superstitions, probably would have agreed that Tertullian reflected public opinion when he said that, for outsiders, conversion made the initiate "an enemy of the public good; of the gods; of public morals," of all that patriotic and religious Romans held sacred.[14] Tertullian knew what had happened during the summer of 202 in his own African city, Carthage, where a twenty-two-year-old aristocrat named Vibia Perpetua, recently married and the mother of an infant son, resolved to undergo baptism along with four other young people, at least two of them slaves. When the magistrate asked whether she was a Christian, she said she was. She was arrested, imprisoned, and sentenced to be torn apart by beasts in the public arena—a death sentence ordinarily reserved for slaves—along with her fellow converts.

Perpetua recorded in her diary what happened when her patrician, gray-haired father arrived at the prison:

While we were under arrest, my father, out of love for me, was trying to persuade me and shake my resolution. "Father," I said, "do you see this vessel, or waterpot, or whatever it is?" "Yes, I do," he said. "Could it be called by any other name than what it is?" I asked; and he said, "No." "Well, so too, I cannot be called anything other than what I am, *Christian*."[15]

Because she was repudiating her family name, Perpetua wrote, "my father was so angry . . . that he started towards me as though he would tear out my eyes; but he left it at that, and departed."[16] A few days later, hoping that his daughter might be given a hearing, Perpetua says, "My father arrived from the city, exhausted with worry, and came to see me to try to persuade me. 'Daughter,'" he said, understandably desperate,

have pity . . . on me, your father, if I deserve to be called your father; if I have loved you more than all your brothers. . . . Do not abandon me to people's scorn. Think of your brothers; think of your mother and your aunt; think of your child, who will not be able to live without you. Give up your pride! You will destroy all of us! None of us will ever be able to speak freely again if anything happens to you.[17]

Perpetua wrote, "My father spoke this way out of love for me, kissing my hands and throwing himself down before me. With tears in his eyes . . . he left me in great sorrow."[18]

Then, on the day when the governor interrogated the prisoners, her father arrived carrying her infant son and continued to plead with her, she says, until the governor "ordered him to be thrown to the ground and beaten with a rod. I felt sorry for father, just as if I myself had been beaten; I grieved for his misery in old age."[19] But Perpetua believed that she now belonged to God's family and maintained her detachment. On the birthday of Emperor Geta, she walked calmly from prison into the amphitheater "as one beloved of God . . . putting down everyone's stare by her own intense gaze,"[20] to die with her new relatives, who included her slave Felicitas as her sister and Revocatus, also a slave, as her brother.

To join the "peculiar Christian society," then, a candidate had to repudiate his or her family, along with its values and practices. Justin Martyr, called "the philosopher," baptized in Rome around the year 140, says that he had come to see himself as one who had been "brought up in bad habits and evil customs"[21] to accept distorted values and worship demons as gods. He tells how he and others had given up promiscuity, magic, greed, wealth, and racial hatred:

We, out of every tribe of people . . . who used to take pleasure in promiscuity, now embrace chastity alone; we, who once had recourse to magic, dedicate ourselves to the good God; we, who valued above everything else acquiring wealth and possessions, now bring what we have into a common fund, and share with everyone in need; we who hated and killed other people, and refused to live with people of another tribe because of their different customs, now live intimately with them.[22]

Every initiate, Justin adds, who "has been convinced, and agreed to our teaching," would pledge to live as a person transformed.

Having changed his or her mind (which is the meaning of the Latin word *paenitentia*) about the past, the candidate could undergo the baptismal "bath" that cleanses away its pollution. The initiate, often shivering beside a river, undressed and went underwater, to emerge wet and naked, "born again." And just as any Roman newborn would first be presented to the father to accept—or reject—before it could be embraced as a member of the family, so the newly baptized would be presented before "God, the Father of all." Now the initiate, no longer called, as before, by his or her paternal name, would hear the initiator pronouncing the name of the "Father of all," of Jesus Christ, and of the holy spirit. Then, clothed in new garments, the reborn Christian would be fed a mixture of milk and honey, the food of newborn infants, and be brought in to greet "those we call brothers and sisters" with a kiss. Now members of the assembled community would invite the newcomer to share bread and wine in the *eucharist* (literally, "thanksgiving"), the sacred family meal. Justin says that believers call baptism "*illumination*, because all who receive it are illuminated in their understanding."[23] These simple, everyday acts—taking off old clothes, bathing, putting on new clothes, then sharing bread and wine—took on, for Jesus' followers, powerful meanings.

As I began sometimes to participate in church services after decades of absence, I experienced the power of worship in new ways. I had grown up nominally Protestant, and thought of ritual as empty form, but now I saw how it could join people of diverse cultures and viewpoints into a single community, and focus and renew their energies. But, apart from these effects, what do such acts mean, and what does it mean to join such a community? These questions are not easy to answer. Many people have tried to impute a single, definitive meaning shared by all "early Christians"; but first-century evidence—much of it from the New Testament—tells a different story.[24] Various groups interpreted baptism in quite different ways; and those who ate bread and drank wine together to celebrate "the Lord's supper" often could not confine the meaning of their worship to any single interpretation.

One of the earliest sources, for example, the Teaching of the Twelve Apostles to the Gentiles, shows that members of certain early groups of Jesus' followers did not think of themselves as *Christians*—as we think of *Christians*—as separate from *Jews*, but as God's people—by which some apparently meant Jews who revered Jesus as the great interpreter of God's law, the Torah. Written in Syria about ten years *before* the New Testament gospels of Matthew and Luke,[25] this writing, known as the Didache (Greek for "teaching"), opens with a succinct summary of God's law, along with a *negative* version of the so-called golden rule: "The Way of Life is this: First, you shall love the God who made you, and your neighbor as yourself; and whatever you do not want to have done to you, do not do to another."[26] The Didache quotes other sayings that Matthew and Luke, writing perhaps about ten years later, will also attribute to Jesus:

> Bless those who curse you; pray for your enemies . . . love those who hate you. . . . If anyone smites you on the right cheek, turn to him the other also. . . . Give to everyone who asks you, and do not refuse

—although its editor adds a prudent warning *not* included in the New Testament: "Let your money sweat in your hands until you know to whom you are giving."[27]

Thus the Didache sets forth what the "way of life" demands, mingling the Ten Commandments with sayings best known to Christians from Jesus' Sermon on the Mount. Like many other pious Jews, the author amplifies these sayings with moral warnings similar to those his contemporaries directed against what they regarded as the everyday crimes of pagan culture, including sex with children, often slave boys, abortion, and killing newborns:

> You shall not kill; you shall not commit adultery; you shall not have sexual intercourse with boys . . . you shall not practice magic; you shall not murder the child in the womb, nor kill newborns . . . you shall not turn away the destitute.[28]

Then, after warning them not to follow the "way of death"— the way especially of the "advocates of the rich," who "turn away the poor and oppress those who suffer, and judge the poor unjustly"—the author, like Jesus in the Gospel of Matthew, urges his hearers to "be perfect." But, *unlike* Matthew, the Didache explains that "being perfect" suggests "bearing the whole yoke of the Lord"—that is, obeying the whole divine law.[29] Also, unlike Matthew, this anonymous follower of Jesus adds, more practically, "If you cannot [be perfect], do what you can."

The historian Jonathan Draper suggests that one early version of the Didache reveals a group of Jesus' followers who were still participating in the life of the Jewish community in their home city in Syria. When members of this group baptized newcomers, they understood baptism as their fellow Jews did then, and still do today: as a "bath" that purifies outsiders—that is, Gentiles—who seek admission to God's people, Israel. The point of this early and influential manual, Draper shows, is to demonstrate how non-Jews may become part of God's people; that is, to offer, just as the title promises, "the teaching of the twelve apostles *to the Gentiles*."[30] The Didache provides these Gentiles an exposition of the "way of life" set forth in the Hebrew Scriptures as Jesus interpreted it, and then shows how Gentiles willing to follow that "way" may be baptized, so that they, too, can share in the blessings of God's coming kingdom.

Finally, the Didache tells how the initiate, who fasts and prays before being baptized, would have learned how sharing in this simple meal of bread and wine links the human family gathered for worship with "God, our Father," and with "Jesus, [his] servant" (or his "child," as the Greek term *pais* may be translated). And by "breaking bread" together, his people celebrate the way God has brought together people who once were scattered, and has joined them as one:

As this broken bread was scattered upon the mountains but was brought together and became one loaf, so let your people be gathered together from the ends of the earth into thy kingdom.[31]

Those speaking this prayer in unison ended by calling—in an ancient Aramaic phrase some Christians invoke to this day—for the imminent coming of the Lord: "Let grace come, and let this world pass away. . . . *Maran atha!* [Our Lord, come!] Amen."[32] According to Draper's analysis, these are Jews who revere Jesus as "God's servant" and believe that his coming signals Israel's restoration at the end of time.

But other early followers of Jesus, like the majority ever since, saw the sacred meal in a much stranger—even macabre—way: as eating human flesh and drinking human blood. Only twenty years after Jesus' death, Paul declared that Jesus himself commanded his followers to do this. Paul, like the gospels of Mark, Matthew, and Luke, tells how, on the night Jesus was betrayed,

> while [the disciples] were eating, [Jesus] took bread, and after blessing it he broke it, gave it to them, and said, "Take: this is my body." Then he took a cup, and after giving thanks he gave it to them, and all of them drank from it, and he said to them, "This is my blood."[33]

Tertullian satirizes the reaction of outsiders to this practice: "We are accused of observing a sacred ritual in which we kill a little child and eat it."[34] He writes,

> No doubt [the Christian] would say, "You must get a child still very young, who does not know what it means to die, and can smile under your knife; and bread to collect the gushing blood. . . . Come, plunge your knife into the infant. . . . Or, if that is someone else's job, simply stand before a human being dying before it has really lived. . . . Take the fresh young blood, saturate your bread with it, and eat freely."[35]

Despite his sarcasm, Tertullian cannot dispel the shocking fact that the Christian "mystery" invites initiates to eat human flesh—even if only symbolically. Pagans might be repelled by the practice of instructing newcomers to drink wine as human blood, but devout Jews, whose very definition of *kosher* (pure) food requires that it be drained of all blood, would be especially disgusted.[36]

But, in their own time, many Jews and Gentiles might have recognized the eucharist as typical of ancient cult worship. Justin Martyr the philosopher worried that pagans would dismiss these rituals with contempt and charge that Christians were simply copying what worshipers in the so-called mystery religions did every day in their exotic cults. Justin admits that the priests who presided over the various temples of "devils"—the gods of Greece, Rome, Egypt, and Asia Minor—often asked their initiates to perform "washings" like baptism, and that priests of the Persian sun god Mithras and the Greek Dionysus "command[ed] the same things to be done" as Jesus allegedly did—even "eating the flesh and drinking the blood" of their god in their sacred meals.[37] But Justin insists that these supposed similarities are actually *imitations* of Christian worship inspired by demons who hope to "deceive and seduce the human race"[38] into thinking that the Christian cult is no different from the mystery cults. Justin might have worried more had he foreseen that, from the fourth century on, Christians would celebrate a new festival—the birthday of Jesus—on December 25, the birthday of the sun god Mithras, around the time of the winter solstice, when the waning sun is reborn as the days grow longer.

Yet the followers of Jesus invoked the mystery cults less than

Jewish tradition as they struggled with a practical—and painful—problem. If Jesus was God's messiah, why did he die such a hideous death? This question troubled Paul himself, who, like many others, wrestled to reconcile the crucifixion with his belief in Jesus' divine mission. In the decades after his death, some followers of Jesus in Jerusalem invoked religious tradition to suggest that, just as animal sacrifices were offered in the Temple, so Jesus had died as a sacrificial offering. And just as those who brought goats, sheep, or bulls to sacrifice afterward feasted on the slain carcasses, so, some suggested, those who benefit from this *human* sacrifice might appropriate its benefits by symbolically "eating" the sacrificial victim. By placing the drama of Jesus' death at the center of their sacred meal, his followers transformed what others would see as total catastrophe—what Paul calls "scandal"[39]—into religious paradox: in the depths of human defeat they claimed to find the victory of God.[40]

Seen this way, Jesus' capture, torture, and death were not, they insisted, simply disastrous. These events had not devastated their hopes, as someone might think who heard what happened from the disciple who concluded ruefully that "we had hoped that he was the one to deliver Israel."[41] Mark insists that Jesus was not captured because his followers lacked the strength to fight for him, after one of them fought with his sword and wounded a member of the arresting party but was routed and fled like the rest. Rather, Mark says, Jesus moved deliberately toward his dreadful death because he recognized that it was somehow "necessary"[42]—but necessary for what?

Mark repeats what some of Jesus' followers in Jerusalem had begun to say—that Jesus foresaw his own death, and voluntarily offered himself as a sacrifice. Giving his disciples bread, he

told them to "take, eat; this is my body."[43] Mark says that after
he had given his disciples wine to drink, he told them, "This is
my blood . . . poured out for many."[44] Matthew invokes the
theme of sacrificial atonement, adding to Mark's account that
Jesus' blood is "poured out for many, *for the forgiveness of sins.*"[45]
Mark and Paul include as well, in different ways, the image of
sacrificial blood ratifying a covenant. Mark looks back to the
covenant of Moses, recalling how Moses threw the blood of sacrificial oxen upon the people, saying, "Behold, the *blood of the
covenant* which the Lord has made with you."[46] So now, Mark
suggests, Jesus anticipates shedding what he calls *"my blood of the
covenant."*[47] But Paul, instead of looking back to the Mosaic covenant, looks forward to the *new*—and better—covenant prophesied by Jeremiah:

> Behold, the days are coming, says the Lord, when I will
> make a *new covenant* with the house of Israel. . . . *Not like the
> covenant which I made with their fathers.* . . . I will put my law
> within them, and I will write it upon their hearts; and I
> will be their God, and they shall be my people . . . and
> they shall all know me . . . and I will remember their sin
> no more.[48]

Thus Paul depicts Jesus offering wine to his disciples with the
words "This cup is the new covenant in my blood."[49]

We do not know for sure whether Jesus actually said these
words. Some historians believe that he must have said something like them; others believe that as his followers struggled to
come to terms with what had happened, and began to reenact
Jesus' "last supper," they formulated these enormously powerful

words. In any case, Jewish tradition suggested a wealth of associations with sacrifice that Paul, Mark, Matthew, and Luke incorporated into various versions of the story.[50] In the process, as we have seen, the sacred meal took on not a single meaning but clusters of meanings that became increasingly rich and complex. Justin tells us what second-century Christians actually did, in various groups he visited as he traveled from Asia Minor to Rome (c. 150 C.E.):

> All those who live in the city or the country gather together in one place on the day of the sun, and the memoirs of the apostles or the writings of the prophets are read. . . . Then we all rise together and pray, and then . . . bread and wine and water are brought[51]

to be shared as Jesus commanded. Christians to this day, including those who do not center their worship on communion, know that how they interpret Jesus' death—whether as sacrifice, and what kind of sacrifice—has much to do with how they understand their faith.

Seen as sacrifice, the meal could suggest not only forgiveness and a new relationship with God but also, like Passover, divine deliverance. Thus Paul recalls how the Passover lamb was slaughtered before the feast and invites his hearers to "the Lord's supper," proclaiming that "Christ, our Passover [lamb], has been sacrificed for us; therefore, let us celebrate the feast."[52] Mark actually writes the Passover feast into the narrative, declaring that Jesus' last supper with his disciples *was* a Passover feast—one that Jesus had carefully, even miraculously, directed his disciples to prepare.[53] Luke and Matthew each expand Mark's version of the story, Luke adding that after the disciples

> prepared the Passover, when the time came, he sat at table, and his apostles with him, and he said to them, "With [great] *desire I have desired to eat this Passover with you* before I suffer; for I tell you, no longer shall I eat it until it is fulfilled in the kingdom of God."[54]

According to Luke and Paul, Jesus not only blessed the bread and wine but also told his followers to "do this in remembrance of me."[55] Thus they imply that, just as Passover recalls how God delivered Israel through Moses, so those who celebrate *this* Passover are to recall simultaneously how God is now delivering his people through Jesus.

The author of the Gospel of John gives a *different* chronology for Jesus' last days, though John, as much as—or even more than—Paul and Luke, nevertheless intends to connect Jesus' death with Passover. However, John writes that "*before* the feast of Passover"[56] Jesus shared a meal with his disciples for the last time, a meal that obviously could not have celebrated Passover. John says that, at that final meal, Jesus washed his disciples' feet—an act which millions of Christians, from Roman Catholic and Orthodox to Baptist or Mormon—have turned into *another* sacrament. But John does *not* tell the story of the last supper that, from the accounts of Paul, Mark, Luke, and Matthew, has shaped Christian worship ever since. Instead, John says that Jesus was arrested on the *previous* night—Thursday—and brought to trial the following morning.

Because John believed that Jesus *became* the Passover lamb, he says that at "about noon, on the day of preparing the Passover"[57]—Friday, the time prescribed for preparing the Passover lamb—Jesus was sentenced to death, tortured, and crucified. Every detail of John's version of Jesus' death dramatizes his conviction that Jesus himself *became* the sacrificial lamb.[58] Thus, to show that Jesus, like the sacrificial Passover lamb, actually died before sunset on the evening of the first day of Passover, John says that a Roman soldier thrust a spear into Jesus' side to make sure that he was dead. At that moment, John says, "out of his side came blood and water,"[59] a physiological observation which also shows how Jesus' sacrifice provides the wine mixed with water that his followers would ritually drink as "his blood."[60] John adds that when the soldiers saw that Jesus was dead, they refrained from breaking his legs, and then he quotes from Exodus that, when preparing the Passover lamb, "you shall not break a bone of [it]."[61] For John, these instructions have become prophecies; thus, he declares, "not a single bone of [Jesus'] body was broken."[62]

Although John omits the story of the last supper itself, he does say that Jesus told his followers to eat his flesh and drink his blood—a suggestion that, he says, offended "the Jews," including many of Jesus' own disciples:

> Jesus said, "I am the living bread which comes down from heaven . . . whoever eats of this bread will live forever; and the bread which I shall give for the life of the world is my flesh."
>
> The Jews then disputed among themselves, saying, "How can this man give us his flesh to eat?"

> So Jesus said to them, "Truly, truly I say to you, unless
> you eat the flesh of the Son of Man and drink his blood,
> you have no life in you. . . . For my flesh is truly food, and
> my blood is truly drink."
> Many of his disciples, when they heard it, said, "This is
> a hard saying; who can listen to it?"[63]

Yet despite the weirdness of such images—and perhaps because
of it—every version of this last supper in the New Testament,
whether by Paul, Mark, Matthew, or Luke, interprets it as a kind
of death-feast, but one that looks forward in hope. So Paul declares that "whenever you eat this bread and drink the cup, *you
proclaim the Lord's death, until he comes.*"[64]

Many Christians *preferred* these powerful images, apparently,
to the more innocuous interpretation found, for example, in Didache; for later generations chose to include in the New Testament the versions of the story that tell of eating flesh and
drinking blood, dying and coming back to life. Yet during the
centuries in which crucifixion remained an immediate and hideous threat, Jesus' followers did not paint a cross—much less a
crucifix—on the walls of the catacombs in Rome as a symbol of
hope. Instead, they depicted Jesus as one who, delivered from
destruction, now delivers others: like Daniel freed from the lions'
den, Jonah released from the belly of the whale, or Lazarus, his
shroud unwinding, walking out of his grave. The Apocalypse
of Peter, one of the so-called gnostic gospels discovered at Nag
Hammadi in Upper Egypt in 1945, goes further, depicting Jesus
"glad and laughing on the cross,"[65] a radiant being of light; and,
as we shall see, the Acts of John, another "heretical" source, depicts Jesus celebrating the eucharist by leading his disciples as

they chant and dance together a mystical hymn, the "Round Dance of the Cross."[66]

Within decades of his death, then, the story of Jesus became for his followers what the Exodus story had become for many generations of Jews: not simply a narrative of past events but a story through which they could interpret their own struggles, their victories, their sufferings, and their hopes. As Jesus and his disciples had traditionally gathered every year to act out the Exodus story at Passover, so his followers, after his death, gathered at Easter to act out the crucial moments of Jesus' story. As Mark tells the story of Jesus, then, he simultaneously offers the script, so to speak, for the drama that his followers are to live out. For just as Mark opens his gospel by telling of Jesus' baptism, so, as we have seen, every newcomer's experience would begin as each is baptized, plunged into water to be "born again" into God's family. And as Mark's account concludes with what happened on "the night Jesus was betrayed," so those who were baptized would gather every week to act out, in their sacred meal, what he said and did that night.

This correspondence helps account, no doubt, for the fact that Mark's gospel—the simplest version of the story later amplified by Matthew and Luke—became the basis for the New Testament gospel canon. Just as Exodus serves as the story line for the Passover ritual, so the story Mark tells came to serve as the story line for the Christian rituals of baptism and the sacred meal.[67] Receiving baptism and gathering every week—or even every day—to share the "Lord's supper," those who participate weave the story of Jesus' life, death, and resurrection into their own lives.[68]

This, then, is what I dimly recognized as I stood in the doorway of the Church of the Heavenly Rest. The drama being played out there "spoke to my condition," as it has to that of millions of people throughout the ages, because it simultaneously acknowledges the reality of fear, grief, and death while—paradoxically—nurturing hope. Four years later, when our son, then six years old, suddenly died, the Church of the Heavenly Rest offered some shelter, along with words and music, when family and friends gathered to bridge an abyss that had seemed impassable.

Such gatherings can also communicate joy—celebrating birth, marriage, or simply, as Paul said, "communion";[69] such worship refracts a spectrum of meaning as varied as the experience of those who participate. Those repenting acts of violence they have done, for example, might find hope for release and forgiveness, while those who have suffered harm might take comfort in the conviction that their sufferings are known to—even shared by—God. Perhaps most often believers experience the shared meal as "communion" with one another and with God; thus when Paul speaks of the "body of Christ," he often means the collective "body" of believers—the union of all who, he says, were "baptized into *one body*, Jews or Greeks, slaves and free, and all were made to drink from one spirit."[70]

Yet, since the fourth century, most churches have required those who would join such communion to profess a complex set of beliefs about God and Jesus—beliefs formulated by fourth-century bishops into the ancient Christian creeds. Some, of course, have no difficulty doing so. Many others, myself included, have had to reflect on what the creeds mean, as well as on what we believe (what does it mean to say that Jesus is the "only Son of God, eternally begotten of the Father," or that "we

believe in one holy catholic and apostolic Church"?). Anyone
with an ear for poetry can hear this creed as a sonorous tone
poem in praise of God and Jesus. Certainly, as a historian, I can
recognize how these creeds came to be part of tradition, and
can appreciate how Constantine, the first Christian emperor,
became convinced that making—and enforcing—such creeds
helped to unify and standardize rival groups and leaders during the turmoil of the fourth century. Yet how do such demands
for belief look today, in light of what we now know about the
origins of the Christian movement?

As we have seen, for nearly three hundred years before these
creeds were written, diverse Christian groups had welcomed
newcomers in various ways. Groups represented by the Didache required those who would join them to embrace the
"way of life" taught by Moses and by Jesus, "God's child." Justin
Martyr the philosopher, now regarded as one of the "fathers of
the church," cared about belief, of course—above all, that the
pagan gods were false, and that one should acknowledge only
the one true God, along with "Jesus Christ, his son"—but what
mattered most was to share—and practice—the values of "God's
people." So, Justin says, "we baptize those" who not only accept Jesus' teaching but *undertake to be able to live accordingly.*[71]
What sustained many Christians, even more than belief, were
stories—above all, shared stories of Jesus' birth and baptism,
and his teachings, his death, and his resurrection. Furthermore,
the astonishing discovery of the gnostic gospels—a cache of ancient secret gospels and other revelations attributed to Jesus
and his disciples—has revealed a much wider range of Christian
groups than we had ever known before.[72] Although later denounced by certain leaders as "heretics," many of these Chris-

tians saw themselves as not so much *believers* as *seekers*, people who "seek for God."

The Church of the Heavenly Rest helped me to realize much that I love about religious tradition, and Christianity in particular—including how powerfully these may affect us, and perhaps even transform us. At the same time, I was also exploring in my academic work the history of Christianity in the light of the Nag Hammadi discoveries, and this research helped clarify what I cannot love: the tendency to identify Christianity with a single, authorized set of beliefs—however these actually vary from church to church—coupled with the conviction that Christian belief alone offers access to God.

Now that scholars have begun to place the sources discovered at Nag Hammadi, like newly discovered pieces of a complex puzzle, next to what we have long known from tradition, we find that these remarkable texts, only now becoming widely known, are transforming what we know as Christianity.[73] As we shall see in the following chapters, we are now beginning to understand these "gospels" much better than we did when I first wrote about them twenty years ago. Let us start by taking a fresh look at the most familiar of all Christian sources—the gospels of the New Testament—in the perspective offered by one of the *other* Christian gospels composed in the first century and discovered at Nag Hammadi, the Gospel of Thomas. As we shall soon see, those who later enshrined the Gospel of John within the New Testament and denounced Thomas's gospel as "heresy" decisively shaped—and inevitably limited—what would become Western Christianity.

↑o↑o↑o↑

GOSPELS IN CONFLICT: JOHN AND THOMAS

I have always read the Gospel of John with fascination, and often with devotion. When I was fourteen, and had joined an evangelical Christian church, I found in the enthusiastic and committed gatherings and in John's gospel, which my fellow Christians treasured, what I then craved—the assurance of belonging to the right group, the true "flock" that alone belonged to God. Like many people, I regarded John as the most spiritual of the four gospels, for in John, Jesus is not only a man but a mysterious, superhuman presence, and he tells his disciples to "love one another."[1] At the time, I did not dwell on disturbing undercurrents—that John alternates his assurance of God's gracious love for those who "believe" with warnings that everyone who "does not believe is condemned already"[2] to eternal death. Nor did I reflect on those scenes in which John says that Jesus spoke of his own people ("the Jews") as if they were alien to him and the devil's offspring.[3]

Before long, however, I learned what inclusion cost: the leaders of the church I attended directed their charges not to associate with outsiders, except to convert them. Then, after a close friend was killed in an automobile accident at the age of sixteen, my fellow evangelicals commiserated but declared that, since he was Jewish and not "born again," he was eternally damned. Distressed and disagreeing with their interpretation—and finding no room for discussion—I realized that I was no longer at home in their world and left that church. When I entered college, I decided to learn Greek in order to read the New Testament in its original language, hoping to discover the source of its power. Reading these terse, stark stories in Greek, I experienced the gospels in a new way, often turning the page to see what happened next, as if I had never read them before. Reading Greek also introduced me firsthand to the poems of Homer, the plays of Sophocles and Aeschylus, Pindar's hymns, and Sappho's invocations; and I began to see that many of these "pagan" writings are also religious literature, but of a different religious sensibility.

After college I studied dance at the Martha Graham School in New York. I loved dance but still wondered what it was about Christianity that I had found so compelling and at the same time so frustrating. I decided to look for the "real Christianity"—believing, as Christians traditionally have, that I might find it by immersing myself in the earliest Christian sources, composed soon after Jesus and his disciples had wandered in Galilee. When I entered the Harvard doctoral program, I was astonished to hear from the other students that Professors Helmut Koester and George MacRae, who taught the early history of Christianity, had file cabinets filled with "gospels" and "apocrypha" written during the first centuries, many of them secret writings of which I'd never heard. These writings, containing sayings, rituals, and dialogues attributed to Jesus and his disciples, were found in 1945 among a cache of texts from the beginning of the Christian era, unearthed near Nag Hammadi in Upper Egypt.[4] When my fellow students and I investigated these sources, we found that they revealed diversity within the Christian movement that later, "official" versions of Christian history had suppressed so effectively that only now, in the Harvard graduate school, did we hear about them. So we asked who wrote these alternative gospels, and when. And how do these relate to—and differ from—the gospels and other writings familiar from the New Testament?

These discoveries challenged us not only intellectually but—in my case at least—spiritually. I had come to respect the work of "church fathers" such as Irenaeus, bishop of Lyons (c. 180), who had denounced such secret writings as "an abyss of madness, and blasphemy against Christ."[5] Therefore I expected these recently discovered texts to be garbled, pretentious, and trivial. Instead I was surprised to find in some of them unexpected spiritual power—in sayings such as this from the Gospel of Thomas, translated by Professor MacRae: "Jesus said: 'If you bring forth what is within you, what you bring forth will save you. If you do not bring forth what is within you, what you do not bring forth will destroy you.' "[6] The strength of this saying is that it does not tell us what to believe but challenges us to discover what lies hidden within ourselves; and, with a shock of recognition, I realized that this perspective seemed to me self-evidently true.

In 1979 I published *The Gnostic Gospels*, a preliminary exploration of the impact of the Nag Hammadi discoveries. Now, about twenty years later, many scholars say that these texts may not be "gnostic"—since many of us are asking what that perplexing term means. Insofar as *gnostic* refers to one who "knows," that is, who seeks experiential insight, it may characterize many of these sources accurately enough; but more often the "church fathers" used the term derisively to refer to those they dismissed as people claiming to "know it all." One thoughtful scholar, Michael Williams, suggests that we should no longer use the term, and another, Karen King, demonstrates its many connotations.[7] Nevertheless, I intended that book to raise certain questions: Why had the church decided that these texts were "heretical" and that only the canonical gospels were "orthodox"? Who made those decisions, and under what conditions? As my colleagues and I looked for answers, I began to understand the political concerns that shaped the early Christian movement.

Thanks to research undertaken since that time and shared by many scholars throughout the world, what that book attempted to offer as a kind of rough, charcoal sketch of the history of Christianity now can be seen as if under an electron microscope—yielding considerably more clarity, detail, and accuracy. What I focus on in this book is how certain Christian leaders from the second century through the fourth came to reject many other sources of revelation and construct instead the New Testament gospel canon of Matthew, Mark, Luke, and John along with the "canon of truth," which became the nucleus of the later creeds that have defined Christianity to this day.

As I worked with many other scholars to edit and annotate these Nag Hammadi texts, we found that this research gradually clarified—and complicated—our understanding of the origins of Christianity. For instead of discovering the purer, simpler "early Christianity" that many of us had been looking for, we found ourselves in the midst of a more diverse and complicated world than any of us could have imagined. For example, many scholars are now convinced that the New Testament Gospel of John, probably written at the end of the first century, emerged from an intense debate over who Jesus was—or is.[8] To my surprise, having spent many months comparing the Gospel of John with the Gospel of Thomas, which may have been written at about the same time, I have now come to see that John's gospel was written in the heat of controversy, to defend certain views of Jesus and to oppose others.

This research has helped clarify not only what John's gospel is *for* but what it is *against.* John says explicitly that he writes "so that you may *believe, and believing, may have life* in [Jesus'] name."[9] What John opposed, as we shall see, includes what the Gospel of Thomas teaches—that God's light shines not only in Jesus but, potentially at least, in everyone. Thomas's gospel encourages the hearer not so much to *believe in Jesus,* as John requires, as to *seek to know God* through one's own, divinely given capacity, since all are created in the image of God. For Christians in later generations, the Gospel of John helped provide a foundation for a unified church, which Thomas, with its emphasis on each person's search for God, did not.

I have also learned after years of study that, although John's gospel is written with great simplicity and power, its meaning is by no means obvious. Even its first generation of readers (c. 90 to 130 C.E.) disagreed about whether John was a true gospel or a false one—and whether it should be part of the New Testament.[10] John's defenders among early Christians revered it as the "*logos* gospel"—the gospel of the divine word or reason (*logos*, in Greek)—and derided those who opposed it as "irrational" (*alogos*, lacking reason). Its detractors, by contrast, were quick to point out that John's narrative differs significantly from those of Matthew, Mark, and Luke. As I compared John with these other gospels, I saw that at certain points this is true, and that some of these differences are much more than variations on a theme.

At crucial moments in its account, for example, John's gospel directly contradicts the combined testimony of the other New Testament gospels. We have seen already that John differs in its version of Jesus' final days; moreover, while Mark, Matthew, and Luke agree that disrupting merchants doing business in the Temple was Jesus' *last* public act, John makes it his *first* act. The three other gospels all say that what finally drove the chief priest and his allies to arrest Jesus was this attack on the money changers, when Jesus in Jerusalem

> entered the temple and began to drive out those who were selling and those who were buying in the temple, and he overturned the tables of the moneychangers and the seats of those who sold doves, and he would not allow anyone to carry anything through the temple.[11]

Mark says of this shocking incident that "when the chief priests and scribes heard of it, they kept looking for a way to kill him,"[12] and Matthew and Luke agree with Mark that the temple authorities had Jesus arrested shortly afterward.

But John places this climactic act at the *beginning* of his story, to suggest that Jesus' whole mission was to purify and transform the worship of God. John also increases the violence of the scene by adding that Jesus "knotted a whip out of small cords" and "drove them all out of the Temple."[13] Unlike the other gospel writers, John mentions no immediate repercussions for this act, probably because, had Jesus been arrested at this point, he would have had no story to tell. To account for Jesus' arrest, John inserts at the end of his narrative a startling story that occurs in none of the other gospels: how Jesus raised his friend Lazarus from the dead, which so alarmed the Jewish authorities that they determined to kill Jesus, and, he adds, the chief priests even "planned to put Lazarus to death as well."[14]

John intends his story of the raising of Lazarus, like his version of the "cleansing of the Temple," to point to deeper meanings. As John tells it, the chief priests had Jesus arrested not because they regarded him as a troublemaker who caused a disturbance in the Temple but because they secretly recognized and feared his power—power that could even raise the dead. John pictures Caiaphas, the high priest, arguing before the Jewish council that "if we let him go on like this, *everyone will believe in him,* and the Romans will come and destroy our holy place and our nation."[15] According to John, such opposition was by no means a matter of the past; even in his own time, about sixty years after Jesus' death, those who opposed Jesus and his followers still feared that "everyone will believe in him." Thus, while John diverges from the other gospels in what he says and how he says it, the brilliant Egyptian teacher named Origen, who lived in the early third century and became one of John's earliest defenders, argues that "although he does not always tell the truth *literally*, he always tells the truth *spiritually*."[16] Origen writes that John's author had constructed a deceptively simple narrative, which, like fine architecture, bears enormous weight.

John's gospel differs from Matthew, Mark, and Luke in a second—and far more significant—way, for John suggests that Jesus is not merely God's human servant but God himself revealed in human form. John says that "the Jews" sought to kill Jesus, accusing him of "making yourself God."[17] But John believed that Jesus actually *is* God in human form; thus he tells how the disciple Thomas finally recognized Jesus when he encountered him risen from the dead and exclaimed, "My Lord and my God!"[18] In one of the earliest commentaries on John (c. 240 C.E.), Origen makes a point of saying that, while the other gospels describe Jesus as *human*, "none of them clearly spoke of his *divinity*, as John does."[19]

But don't the other gospels also say that Jesus is God? Don't Matthew and Mark, for example, call Jesus "son of God," and doesn't this mean that Jesus is virtually—almost *genetically*—the same as God? Like most people who grow up familiar with Christian tradition, I assumed that all the gospels say the same thing or, at most, offer variations on a single theme. Because Matthew, Mark, and Luke share a similar perspective, scholars call these gospels synoptic (literally, "seeing together"). Only in graduate school, when I investigated each gospel, so far as possible, in its historical context, did I see how radical is John's claim that Jesus is God manifest in human form.

Although Mark and the other evangelists use titles that Christians today often take as indicating Jesus' divinity, such as "son of

God" and "messiah," in Mark's own time these titles designated *human* roles.[20] The Christians who translated these titles into English fifteen centuries later believed they showed that Jesus was uniquely related to God, and so they capitalized them—a linguistic convention that does not occur in Greek. But Mark's contemporaries would most likely have seen Jesus as a *man*—although one gifted, as Mark says, with the power of the holy spirit, and divinely appointed to rule in the coming kingdom of God.

Yet as we shall see, after the gospels of Mark, Matthew, and Luke were joined with John's gospel and Paul's letters to become the "New Testament"—a process that took place over some two hundred years (c. 160 to 360 C.E.)—most Christians came to read these earlier gospels through John's lens, and thus to find in all of them evidence of John's conviction that Jesus is "Lord and God."[21] The gospels discovered in 1945 in Upper Egypt, however, offer different perspectives. For if Matthew, Mark, and Luke had been joined with the Gospel of Thomas instead of with John, for example, or had *both* John and Thomas been included in the New Testament canon, Christians probably would have read the first three gospels quite differently. The gospels of Thomas and John speak for different groups of Jesus' followers engaged in discussion, even argument, toward the end of the first century. What they debated is this: Who is Jesus, and what is the "good news" (in Greek *euangellion*, "gospel") about him?

The Gospel of Thomas contains teaching venerated by "Thomas Christians," apparently an early group that, like those devoted to Luke, Matthew, and John, thrived during the first century. What astonished scholars when they first read Thomas, in the 1940s, was that, although it contains many sayings of Jesus that Luke and Matthew also include in their gospels, it contains *other* sayings that apparently derive from a tradition different from that of the synoptic gospels.[22] Although we do not know where the Gospel of Thomas was written, many scholars, noting names associated with Syria, think that it originated there. The Acts of Thomas (c. 200 C.E.), probably written in Syriac, claims that Thomas himself evangelized India,[23] and to this day there are Thomas Christians in India who call Thomas the founder of their faith. Although Mark, Matthew, and Luke mention him among "the twelve" apostles, Thomas is not a proper name but means "twin" in Aramaic, the language that Jesus would have spoken. As Professor Helmut Koester shows, although this disciple was called by his Aramaic nickname, the gospel itself explains that his given name was Judas (but, his admirers specify, "not Iscariot"). Since this disciple was known by the name of Thomas, both the Gospel of Thomas and the Gospel of John also translate Thomas into Greek, explaining to their Greek readers that this disciple is "the one called 'Didymus,'" the Greek term for "twin."[24]

As we shall see, John probably knew what the Gospel of Thomas taught—if not its actual text. Many of the teachings in the Gospel of John that differ from those in Matthew and Luke sound much like sayings in the Gospel of Thomas: in fact, what first impressed scholars who compared these two gospels is how similar they are. Both John and Thomas, for example, apparently assume that the reader already knows the basic story Mark and the others tell, and each claims to go beyond that story and reveal what Jesus taught his disciples in private. When, for example, John tells what happened on the night that Judas betrayed Jesus, he inserts into his account nearly *five chapters* of teaching unique to his gospel—the so-called farewell discourses of John 13 through 18, which consist of intimate dialogue between the disciples and Jesus, as well as a great deal of monologue. Similarly, the Gospel of Thomas, as we noted, claims to offer "secret sayings, which the living Jesus spoke," and adds that "Didymus Judas Thomas wrote them down."[25]

John and Thomas give similar accounts of what Jesus taught privately. Unlike Matthew, Mark, and Luke, who say that Jesus warned of the coming "end of time," both John and Thomas say that he directed his disciples instead toward the beginning of time—to the creation account of Genesis 1—and identify Jesus with the divine light that came into being "in the beginning."[26] Thomas and John both say that this primordial light connects Jesus with the entire universe, since, as John says, "all things were made through the word [logos; or, the light]."[27] Professor Koester has noted such similarities in detail, and concludes that these two authors drew upon common sources.[28] While Mark, Matthew, and Luke identify Jesus as God's human agent, John and Thomas characterize him instead as God's own light in human form.

Yet, despite these similarities, the authors of John and Thomas take Jesus' private teaching in sharply different directions. For John, identifying Jesus with the light that came into being "in the beginning" is what makes him unique—God's "only begotten son." John calls him the "light of all humanity,"[29] and believes that Jesus alone brings divine light to a world otherwise sunk into darkness. John says that we can experience God only through the divine light embodied in Jesus. But certain passages in Thomas's gospel draw a quite different conclusion: that the divine light Jesus embodied is shared by humanity, since we are all made "in the image of God."[30] Thus Thomas expresses what would become a central theme of Jewish—and later Christian—mysticism a thousand years later: that the "image of God" is hidden within everyone, although most people remain unaware of its presence.

What might have been complementary interpretations of God's presence on earth became, instead, rival ones; for by claiming that Jesus alone embodies the divine light, John challenges Thomas's claim that this light may be present in everyone. John's views, of course, prevailed, and have shaped Christian thought ever since. For after John's teaching was collected along with three other gospels into the New Testament, his view of Jesus came to dominate and even to define what we *mean* by Christian teaching. Some Christians who championed the "fourfold gospel"[31]—Matthew, Mark, Luke, and John—of the New Testament denounced the kind of teaching found in the Gospel of Thomas (along with many other writings that they called "secret and illegitimate")[32] and called upon believers to cast out such teaching as *heresy*. How this happened, and what it means for the history of Christian tradition, is what this work will explore.

To appreciate the tremendous leap that John—and Thomas—took, let us recall how the gospels of Mark, Matthew, and Luke characterize Jesus. The earliest of these gospels, Mark, written about forty years after Jesus' death (c. 70 C.E.), presents, as its central mystery, the question of who Jesus is. Mark tells how Jesus' disciples discussed—and discovered—the secret of his identity:

> And Jesus went on with his disciples to the villages of Caesarea Philippi; and on the way he asked his disciples,

"Who do people say that I am?" And they told him, "John the Baptist; and others say, Elijah; and others, one of the prophets." And he asked them, "But who do you say that I am?" Peter answered him, "You are the messiah."[33]

Then Mark immediately shows how Peter, although rightly seeing Jesus as God's *messiah*, literally "anointed one"—the man designated to be Israel's future king—does not understand what is going to happen. When Jesus explains that he must suffer and die, Peter protests in shock, since he expects God's "anointed one" not to die but to be crowned and enthroned in Jerusalem.

At the desolate scene of the crucifixion, Mark tells how Jesus cried out that God had abandoned him, uttered a final, inarticulate cry, and died; yet a Roman centurion who watched him die declared, "Truly, this man was a son of God."[34] Although to a non–Jew like the centurion, "son of God" might have indicated a divine being, Jesus' earliest followers, like Mark, were Jewish and understood that "son of God," like "messiah," designated Israel's human king. During Israel's ancient coronation ceremonies, the future king was anointed with oil to show God's favor while a chorus singing one of the ceremonial psalms proclaimed that when the king is crowned he becomes God's representative, his human "son."[35] Thus when Mark opens his gospel saying that "this is the gospel of Jesus, the *messiah*, the *son of God*,"[36] he is announcing that God has chosen Jesus to be the future king of Israel. Since Mark writes in Greek, he translates the Hebrew term *messiah* as *christos* ("anointed one" in Greek), which later becomes, in English, "Jesus [the] christ."

In Mark, Jesus also characterizes himself as "son of man," the meaning of which is ambiguous. Often in the Hebrew Bible, "son of man" means nothing more than "human being" (in Hebrew, *ben adam* means "son of Adam"). The prophet Ezekiel, for example, says that the Lord repeatedly addressed him as "son of man," often translated "mortal";[37] thus when Mark's Jesus calls himself "son of man," he too may simply mean "human being." Yet Mark's contemporaries who were familiar with the Hebrew Bible may also have recognized "son of man" as referring to the mysterious person whom the prophet Daniel saw in a vision appearing before God's throne to be invested with power:

> I saw in the night visions, and behold, coming with the clouds of heaven was one like a *son of man*, and he came to the Ancient of Days and was presented before him. And to him was given dominion and glory, and kingdom, so that all peoples, nations, and languages should serve him . . . an everlasting dominion, which shall not pass away.[38]

Mark says that when the high priest interrogated Jesus at his trial, and asked, "Are you the messiah, the son of God?" Jesus answered, "I am; and you will see the son of man . . . 'coming with the clouds of heaven.' "[39] According to Mark, then, Jesus not only claimed the royal titles of Israel's king ("messiah," "son of God") but actually quoted Daniel's vision to suggest that he—or perhaps someone else whose coming he foresaw—was the "son of man" whom the prophet saw appearing before God's throne in heaven. Matthew and Luke follow Mark in describing Jesus both as a future king ("messiah," "son of God") and as a mortal invested with divine power ("son of man").

None of these titles, however, explains precisely who Jesus is. Instead, the gospel writers invoke a cluster of traditional terms to express their radical conviction that Jesus of Nazareth was a man raised to unique—even supernatural—status. Luke suggests, however, that it was only after Jesus' death that God, in an unprecedented act of favor, restored him to life, and thus *promoted* Jesus, so to speak, not only to "messiah" but also to "Lord"—a name that Jewish tradition ordinarily reserves strictly for the divine Lord himself. According to Luke's account, written ten to twenty years after Mark's, Peter dares announce to the "men of Jerusalem" that Jesus alone, of the entire human race, returned alive after death, and that this proves that "God *has made him both Lord and messiah*—this Jesus whom you crucified."[40]

Yet John, who wrote about a decade after Luke, opens his gospel with a poem which suggests that Jesus is not human at all but the divine, eternal Word of God in human *form* ("in the beginning was the word, and the word was with God, and the word was God").[41] The author whom we call John probably knew that he was not the first—and certainly not the only—Christian to believe that Jesus was somehow divine. Some fifty years earlier, the apostle Paul, probably quoting an early hymn, had said of Jesus that

> although *he was in the form of God, he did not count equality with God as a thing to be grasped,* but emptied himself, *taking the form of a servant, being found in the likeness of a human being.*[42]

Unlike Luke, who depicts Jesus as a man raised to divine status, John, as does the hymn Paul quotes, pictures him instead as a divine being who descended to earth—temporarily—to take on human *form*. Elsewhere, Paul declares that it is the holy spirit who inspires those who believe that "Jesus is Lord!"[43] Sixty years later, one of Paul's admirers, the Syrian bishop Ignatius of Antioch, anticipating his impending martyrdom, wrote that he passionately longed to "imitate the suffering of my God"[44]—that is, of Jesus. So Pliny, the Roman governor of Bithynia in Asia Minor, probably was right when, after investigating suspicious persons in his province, he wrote to the emperor Trajan (c. 115) that these Christians "sing a hymn to Jesus as to a god"[45]—perhaps it was the same hymn that Paul knew.

This is why some historians, having compared the Gospel of Mark (written 68 to 70 c.e.) with the gospels of Matthew and Luke (c. 80 to 90), and then with that of John (c. 90 to 100), have thought that John's gospel represents a transition from a lower to a higher Christology—an increasingly elevated view of Jesus. These historians point out that such views developed from the first century on and culminated in phrases like those enshrined in the Nicene Creed, which proclaim Jesus to be "God from God, Light from Light, true God from true God."

Yet Christian teaching about Jesus does not follow a simple evolutionary pattern. Although John's formulations have virtually defined orthodox Christian doctrine for nearly two thousand years, they were not universally accepted in his own time. And while the claims of Jesus' divinity by Paul and John surpass those of Mark, Luke, and Matthew, Thomas's gospel, written perhaps around the same time as John's, takes similar language to mean something quite different. Because the Gospel of Thomas diverges from the more familiar pattern found in John, let us look at it first.

We should note that, although I am using here the traditional names, Thomas and John, and the traditional term *author*, no one knows who actually wrote either gospel. Some scholars have observed that whoever assembled the sayings that constitute the Gospel of Thomas may have been less an author than a compiler—or several compilers—who, rather than *composing* these sayings, simply *collected* traditional sayings and wrote them down.[46] In Thomas's gospel, then, as in John, Matthew, and Luke, we sometimes find sayings that seem to contradict each other. For example, both John and Thomas include some sayings suggesting that those who come to know God are very few—a chosen few. Such sayings echo traditional teaching about divine election, and teach that God chooses those who are able to know him;[47] while the cluster of sayings I take as the key to interpreting Thomas suggest instead that everyone, in creation, receives an innate capacity to know God. We know almost nothing about the person we call Thomas, except that, like the evangelists who wrote the gospels of the New Testament, he wrote in the name of a disciple, apparently intending to convey "the gospel" as this disciple taught it. As we noted, then, Thomas apparently assumes that his hearers are already familiar with Mark's story of how Peter discovered the secret of Jesus' identity, that "you are the messiah." When Matthew repeats this story, he adds that Jesus blessed Peter for the accuracy of his recognition: "Blessed are you, Simon Bar Jonas; it was not a human being who revealed this to you, but my Father in heaven."[48]

Thomas tells the same story differently. According to Thomas, when Jesus asks, "Who am I?" he receives not one but three responses from various disciples. Peter first gives, in effect, the same answer as he does in the gospels of Mark and Matthew: "You are like a *righteous messenger*," a phrase that may interpret the He-

brew term *messiah* ("anointed one") for the Greek-speaking audience whom Thomas addresses. The disciple Matthew answers
next: "You are like a *wise philosopher*"—a phrase perhaps intended
to convey the Hebrew term *rabbi* ("teacher") in language any
Gentile could understand. (This disciple is the one traditionally
believed to have written the Gospel of Matthew, which, more
than any other, depicts Jesus as a rabbi.) But when a third disciple, Thomas himself, answers Jesus' question, his response con-
founds the other two: "Master, my mouth is wholly incapable
of saying whom you are like." Jesus replies, "I am not your master, because you have drunk, and have become drunk from
the same stream which I measured out."[49] Jesus does not deny
what Peter and Matthew have said but implies that their answers represent inferior levels of understanding. Then he takes
Thomas aside and reveals to him alone three sayings so secret
that they cannot be written down, even in this gospel filled
with "secret sayings":

> Jesus took Thomas and withdrew, and told him three
> things. When Thomas returned to his companions, they
> asked him, "What did Jesus say to you?" Thomas said, "If I
> tell you even one of the things which he told me, you will
> pick up stones and throw them at me; and a fire will come
> out of the stones and burn you up."[50]

Though Thomas does not reveal here what these "secret words"
are for which the others might stone him to death for blasphemy, he does imply that these secrets reveal more about
Jesus and his message than *either* Peter or Matthew understands.
    What then is the gospel—the "good news"—according to

Thomas, and how does it differ from what is told in the synoptic gospels of Mark, Matthew, and Luke? Mark opens his gospel
when Jesus announces "the good news of the kingdom of God,"
and Mark tells how Jesus, baptized by John, sees "the heavens
torn apart" and God's spirit descending upon him.[51] Immediately afterward, having been driven by God's spirit into the
wilderness to contend against Satan, Jesus returns triumphantly
to announce his first, urgent message: "The kingdom of God is
coming near: repent, and believe in the gospel."[52] According to
Mark, Jesus teaches that this kingdom will come during the lifetime of his disciples: "There are some of you standing here who
will not taste death until you see the kingdom of God come in
power!"[53] Later, in Jerusalem, where his disciples admire the
gleaming walls of the great Temple, Jesus asks, "Do you see
these great stones? Not one stone will be left here upon another; all will be torn down."[54]

Hearing Jesus announce the coming kingdom of God—an
earth-shattering event that is about to transform the world—
Peter, James, John, and Andrew ask privately when these things
will happen. Jesus does not name the day but tells them the
"signs of the times" that will signal its approach. He predicts that
"wars and rumors of wars," earthquakes, and famine will initiate "the birth pangs of the messiah," and warns his followers to
expect to be "beaten in synagogues," arraigned before "gover-
nors and kings," betrayed by family members, and "hated by
all." Still worse: the great Temple in Jerusalem will be desecrated
and ruined, floods of refugees will flee the city—"such suffering
as has not been from the beginning of creation . . . until now,
and no, never will be."[55] Still later, Mark says, Jesus predicted that
"the sun will be darkened, and the moon will not give light; stars

will fall from heaven" as people see in the sky supernatural events foreseen by the prophet Daniel, who told of the " 'Son of man coming in the clouds' with great power and glory."[56] Solemnly Jesus warns his disciples that "truly, I tell you, this generation will not pass away until all these things have taken place"; above all, he warns, "Keep awake."[57]

But according to both the Gospel of Thomas and the Gospel of John, Jesus reveals that the kingdom of God, which many believers, including Mark, expect in the future, not only is "coming" but is already here—an immediate and continuing spiritual reality. According to John, Jesus announces that the Day of Judgment, which the prophets call "the day of the Lord," "is coming, *and is now*,"[58] and adds that the "resurrection of the dead" also may happen now. For when Jesus consoles his friends Mary and Martha on the death of their brother Lazarus and asks whether they believe he will rise from the dead, Martha repeats the hope of the pious, saying, "I know that he will rise in the resurrection on the last day."[59] But in John, Jesus astonishes everyone as he immediately proceeds to raise Lazarus, four days dead, calling him forth alive from his grave. Thus the great transformation expected at the end of time can—and does—happen here and now.

According to the Gospel of Thomas, the "living Jesus" himself challenges those who mistake the kingdom of God for an otherworldly place or a future event:

Jesus said, "If those who lead you say to you, 'Look, the kingdom is in the sky,' then the birds of the sky will get there before you. . . . If they say to you, 'It is in the sea,' then the fish will get there before you."[60]

Here Thomas's Jesus ridicules certain unnamed leaders—perhaps even Peter himself, or his disciple Mark; for it is in Mark that the troubled disciples ask Jesus what to look for as "signs of the end," and Jesus takes them seriously, warning of ominous events to come, and concludes by admonishing them to "watch."[61] But Thomas claims that Jesus spoke differently in secret:

> His disciples said to him, "When will the resurrection of the dead come, and when will the new world come?" He said to them, "What you look forward to has already come, but you do not recognize it."[62]

When they ask again, "When will the kingdom come?" Thomas's Jesus says,

> "It will not come by waiting for it. It will not be a matter of saying, 'Here it is,' or 'There it is.' Rather, the kingdom of the Father is spread out upon the earth, and people do not see it."[63]

The Gospel of Luke includes passages suggesting that other believers agree with Thomas that the kingdom of God is somehow present here and now; in fact, Luke offers an alternate version of the same saying:

> Being asked by the Pharisees when the kingdom of God was coming, [Jesus] answered them, "The kingdom of God is not coming with signs that can be observed, nor will they say, 'Look, here it is!' or 'There it is!,' for the kingdom of God is within you."[64]

Some have taken the phrase "within you" to mean that the kingdom is among the disciples so long as Jesus is with them, while
others take it to mean that the kingdom of God is embodied not
only in Jesus but in everyone. The New Revised Standard Version of the Bible adopts the first sense—that Jesus alone embodies the kingdom of God. But a century ago, in a book called
The Kingdom of God Is Within You, Leo Tolstoy urged Christians to
give up coercion and violence in order to realize God's kingdom
here and now. Thomas Merton, the twentieth-century writer and
Trappist monk, agreed with Tolstoy but interpreted the kingdom
of God mystically rather than practically.[65]

In certain passages, then, the Gospel of Thomas interprets the
kingdom of God as Tolstoy and Merton would do nearly two
thousand years later. The Gospel of Mary Magdalene, also discovered in Egypt, but in 1896, about fifty years before the Nag
Hammadi find, echoes this theme: Jesus tells his disciples, "Let
no one lead you astray, saying, 'Lo, here!' or 'Lo, there!' For the
Son of Man is within you. Follow after him!"[66] Yet after including his version of this saying at one point in his gospel, Luke re-
treats from this position and concludes his account with the
kind of apocalyptic warnings found in Mark: the Son of Man is
not a divine presence in all of us but a terrifying judge who is
coming to summon everyone to the day of wrath that, Luke's
Jesus warns, may

> catch you unexpectedly, like a trap; for it will come upon
> all who live upon the face of the whole earth. Be alert at
> all times, and pray that you may have the strength to es-
> cape all these things that will happen, and to stand before
> the Son of Man.[67]

The Gospels of Thomas and John, however, speak for those who understand Jesus' message quite differently. Both say that, instead of warning his disciples about the *end of time*, Jesus points them toward the *beginning*. John opens with the famous prologue describing the beginning of the universe, when "the word was with God, and the word was God."[68] John is referring, of course, to the opening verses of Genesis: "in the beginning" there was a vast, formless void, darkness, and "the abyss," or deep water, and "a wind [or spirit] from God swept over the face of the waters."[69] Yet before there were sun, moon, or stars, there was, first of all, light: "And God said, 'Let there be light,' and there was light."[70] Thus John identifies Jesus not only with the *word* that God spoke but also with the divine *light* that it called into being—what he calls "the true light that enlightens everyone, coming into the world."[71]

Thomas's Jesus also challenges those who persist in asking him about the "end time": "Have you found the beginning, then, that you look to the end?" Here, too, he directs them to go back to the beginning, "for whoever takes his place in the beginning will know the end, and will not taste death"[72]—that is, will be restored to the luminous state of creation before the fall. Thomas, like John, identifies Jesus with the light that existed before the dawn of creation. According to Thomas, Jesus says that this primordial light not only brought the entire universe into being but still shines through everything we see and touch. For this primordial light is not simply impersonal energy but a being that speaks with a human voice—with *Jesus'* voice:

Jesus said, "I am the light which is before all things. It is I who am all things. From me all things came forth, and to me all things extend. Split a piece of wood, and I am there; lift up the stone, and you will find me."[73]

Yet, despite similarities between John's and Thomas's versions of Jesus' secret teaching, when we look more closely, we begin to see that John's understanding of Jesus' "way" is diametrically opposed to Thomas's on the practical and crucial question: How can we find that light? Let us look first at the Gospel of Thomas.

Thomas's gospel offers only cryptic clues—not answers—to those who seek the way to God. Thomas's "living Jesus" challenges his hearers to find the way for themselves: "Jesus said, 'Whoever finds the interpretation of these words will not taste death,' "[74] and he warns the disciples that the search will disturb and astonish them: "Jesus said, 'Let the one who seeks not stop seeking until he finds. When he finds, he will become troubled; when he becomes troubled, he will be astonished and will rule over all things."[75] Thus here again Jesus encourages those who seek by telling them that they already have the internal resources they need to find what they are looking for: "Jesus said, 'If you bring forth what is within you, what you bring forth will save you. If you do not bring forth what is within you, what you do not bring forth will destroy you.' "[76]

Yet the "disciples [still] questioned him," Thomas writes, "saying, 'Do you want us to fast? How should we pray? Should we give alms? What diet should we observe?' "[77] In Matthew and Luke, Jesus responds to such questions with practical, straightforward answers. For example, he instructs them that "when you give alms, do not let your left hand know what your right hand is doing, so that your alms may be done in secret."[78] When you fast, "put oil on your head, and wash your face."[79] And "when you pray, pray like this, [saying], 'Our Father, who art in heaven. . . .' "[80] In Thomas, Jesus gives no such instructions. Instead, when his disciples ask him what to do—how to pray, what to eat, whether to fast or give money, he answers only with another *koan:* "Do not tell lies, and do not do what you hate; for all things are plain in the sight of heaven."[81] In other words, the capacity to discover the truth is within you. When the disciples still demand that Jesus "tell us who you are, so that we may believe in you," he again deflects the question and directs them to see for themselves: "He said to them, 'You read the face of the sky and the earth, but you have not recognized the one who stands before you, and you do not know how to read this present moment.' "[82] Plotinus, an Alexandrian philosopher baffled and apparently irritated by such sayings, complained that "they are always saying to us, 'Look to God!' But they do not tell us *where* or *how* to look."[83]

Yet Thomas's Jesus offers some clues. After dismissing those who expect the future coming of the kingdom of God, as countless Christians have always done and still do, Thomas's Jesus declares that

> the Kingdom is inside you, and outside you. When you come to know yourselves, then you will be known, and you will see that it is you who are the children of the living Father. But if you will not know yourselves, you dwell in poverty, and it is you who *are* that poverty.[84]

This cryptic saying raises a further question: *How* can we know ourselves? According to Thomas, Jesus declares that we must find out first where we came from, and go back and take our place "in the beginning." Then he says something even stranger: "Blessed is the one who came into being before he came into being."[85] But how can one go back before one's own birth—or even before human creation? What *was* there before human creation—even before the creation of the universe?

According to Genesis, "in the beginning" there was, first of all, the primordial light. For Thomas this means that in creating *"adam* [humankind] in his image," as Genesis 1:26 says, God created us in the image of the primordial light. Like many other readers of Genesis, then and now, Thomas suggests that what appeared in the primordial light was "a human being, very marvelous," a being of radiant light, the prototype of the human Adam, whom God created on the sixth day. This "light Adam," although human in form, is simultaneously, in some mysterious way, also divine.[86] Thus Jesus suggests here that we have spiritual resources within us precisely because we were made "in the image of God." Irenaeus, the Christian bishop of Lyons (c. 180), warns his flock to despise "heretics" who speak like this, and who "call humankind [*anthropos*] the God of all things, also calling him *light*, and *blessed*, and *eternal.*"[87] But, as we noted, what Irenaeus here dismisses as heretical later became a central theme of Jewish mystical tradition—that the "image of God" is hidden within each of us, secretly linking God and all humankind.[88]

Thus Thomas's Jesus tells his disciples that not only *he* comes forth from divine light but so do we all:

If they say to you, "Where did you come from?" say to them, "*We came from the light, the place where the light came into being by itself,* and was revealed through their image." If they say to you, "Who are you?" say, "We are its children, the chosen of the living father."[89]

According to Thomas, Jesus rebukes those who seek access to God elsewhere, even—perhaps especially—those who seek it by trying to "follow Jesus" himself. When certain disciples plead with Jesus to "show us the place where *you* are, since it is necessary for us to seek it," he does not bother to answer so misguided a question and redirects the disciples away from themselves toward the light hidden within each person: "There is light within a person of light, and it lights up the whole universe. If it does not shine, there is darkness."[90] In other words, one either discovers the light within that illuminates "the whole universe" or lives in darkness, within and without.

But discovering the divine light within is more than a matter of being told that it is there, for such vision shatters one's identity: "When you see your likeness [in a mirror] you are pleased; but when you see your images, which have come into being before you, how much will you have to bear!"[91] Instead of self-gratification, one finds the terror of annihilation. The poet Rainer Maria Rilke gives a similar warning about encountering the divine, for "every angel is terrifying." Giving oneself over to such an encounter, he says, involves terror, as if such an angel

> would come more fiercely to interrogate you,
> and rush to seize you blazing like a star,
> and bend you as if trying to create you,
> and break you open, out of who you are.[92]

What "breaks [us] open, out of who [we] are," shatters the ways in which we ordinarily identify ourselves, by gender, name, ethnic origin, social status. So, Thomas adds, "Jesus said, 'Let the one who seeks not stop seeking until he finds. When he finds, he will become troubled. When he becomes troubled, he will be astonished.'"[93]

Finally Jesus reveals to Thomas that "whoever drinks from my mouth will become as I am, and I myself will become that person, and the mysteries shall be revealed to him."[94] This, I believe, is the symbolic meaning of attributing this gospel to Thomas, whose name means "twin." By encountering the "living Jesus," as Thomas suggests, one may come to recognize oneself and Jesus as, so to speak, identical twins. In the Book of Thomas the Contender, another ancient book belonging to Syrian Thomas tradition discovered at Nag Hammadi, "the living Jesus" addresses Thomas (and, by implication, the reader) as follows:

Since you are my twin and my true companion, examine yourself, and learn who you are. . . . Since you will be called my [twin], . . . although you do not understand it yet . . . you will be called "the one who knows himself." For whoever has not known himself knows nothing, but whoever has known himself has simultaneously come to know the depth of all things.[95]

I was amazed when I went back to the Gospel of John after reading Thomas, for Thomas and John clearly draw upon similar language and images, and both, apparently, begin with similar "secret teaching." But John takes this teaching to mean something so different from Thomas that I wondered whether John could have written his gospel to refute what Thomas teaches. For months I investigated this possibility, and explored the work of other scholars who also have compared these sources, and I was finally convinced that this is what happened. As the scholar Gregory Riley points out, John—and only John—presents a challenging and critical portrait of the disciple he calls "Thomas, the one called Didymus,"[96] and, as Riley suggests, it is John who invented the character we call *Doubting* Thomas, perhaps as a way of caricaturing those who revered a teacher—and a version of Jesus' teaching—that he regarded as faithless and false. The writer called John may have met Thomas Christians among people he knew in his own city—and may have worried that their teaching would spread to Christian groups elsewhere. John probably knew that certain Jewish groups—as well as many pagans who read and admired Genesis 1—also taught that the "image of God" was within humankind; in any case, John decided to write his own gospel insisting that it is Jesus—and only Jesus—who embodies God's word, and therefore speaks with divine authority.

Who, then, wrote the Gospel of John? Although we cannot answer this question with certainty, the text itself provides some clues. The author we call John was probably a Jewish follower of Jesus who, various scholars suggest, may have lived in Ephesus or in Antioch, the capital of Syria, and probably wrote toward the end of the first century (c. 90 to 100 C.E.).[97] Some scholars suggest that, as a young man, before mid-century, he may have been attracted to the circle gathered around John the Baptist, as was Jesus of Nazareth, who also came to hear John preach, and received baptism from him in the Jordan River, which the Baptist John promised would prepare people for the coming day of divine judgment. At some point—perhaps after King Herod beheaded the Baptist—this other John may have followed Jesus. His account shows his familiarity with Judaea and its local Jewish practices, and includes details which suggest that he traveled with Jesus and his other disciples during their last journey to Jerusalem, as he claims to have done.

The conclusion added by John to the gospel implies that after that time John lived so long that some of Jesus' followers hoped that the kingdom of God would come during his lifetime, and so that he would never die.[98] According to church tradition, John lived as an old man in Ephesus, revered as the spiritual leader of a circle of Jesus' followers—a passionate, articulate man, educated in Jewish tradition and by no means provincial. Like many other Jews of his time, John was influenced by Greek philosophic and religious ideas. But, if this surmise is true—which I regard as possible, although not likely—his old age must have been a stormy time, for he would have been excluded from his home synagogue and threatened by Roman persecution. Thus John contended not only against hostile outsiders but also with other Jews—including other groups of Jesus' followers.

From the second century to the present, most Christians have assumed that the author of this gospel was in fact the John who was the brother of James, whom Jesus saw mending nets with their father, Zebedee, and called to himself—one of those who "immediately left the boat and their father, and followed him."[99] In that case, John would be one of the group called "the twelve," headed by Peter. Yet the gospel itself (and its possibly added conclusion) declares that it was written by "the disciple whom Jesus loved." If John, the son of Zebedee, was that "beloved disciple," why does his name never appear in the gospel, and why does the gospel never mention either "the apostles" or "the twelve"? If the author had been one of them, why doesn't he say so? Why, while acknowledging Peter as a leader, does he simultaneously denigrate Peter's leadership in favor of the "beloved disciple" and claim that this—otherwise anonymous—disciple's greater authority ensures the truth of his gospel? Could a fisherman from Galilee have written the elegant, spare, philosophically sophisticated prose of this gospel?

Two generations of scholars have devoted hundreds of articles and monographs to such questions, and have proposed various solutions. Some suggest that the author was a different John, "John the elder," a follower of Jesus from Ephesus, whom Christians in later generations confused with John the apostle; others say that the disciple John was the witness whose authority stood behind the gospel but was not its actual author; still others believe that the author was an anonymous leader of a lesser-known circle of disciples, distinct from "the twelve."

Furthermore, while the author of this gospel accepts Peter's authority and his teaching, he also claims that the "beloved disciple" surpasses Peter. So while John pictures Peter as one of Jesus' first disciples, he does *not* repeat the story that Mark, Matthew, and Luke so prominently featured, in which Peter first recognized Jesus—the story that Mark, and many Christians to this day, take to mean that Peter was the disciples' leader, and the church's founder. Moreover, Matthew adds that Jesus promised Peter would succeed him as the founding "rock" upon which the future church would stand[100]—a statement many later took to mean that Peter stood first in the apostolic succession and was the spiritual ancestor of all subsequent popes. Matthew's gospel, like Mark's and Luke's, apparently reflects the view of the so-called Peter Christians—a group based in Rome. Yet all four gospels that eventually formed the New Testament either endorsed Peter's leadership—as Matthew, Mark, and Luke did— or at least grudgingly accepted it—as John did. From the mid-second century, this group, which called themselves catholic (literally, "universal"), remain the founders with whom Roman Catholic and most Protestant Christians identify.

But not all first-century Christians agreed that Jesus named Peter as his primary successor, or identified with that founding group. The gospel we call by John's name insists, on the contrary, that no one—not even Peter—knew Jesus as well as "the disciple whom Jesus loved,"[101] the mysterious, unnamed disciple who is usually assumed to be John himself. Though John acknowledges Peter's importance by featuring him often in his narrative, he always places him second to this "disciple, whom Jesus loved," who, he says, actually witnessed the events he records. For example, John tells how "the disciple whom Jesus loved" reclined next to Jesus at the last meal he shared with his disciples and dared ask him directly—as Peter did not—who would betray him.[102] John adds that even after Judas, and then Peter, betrayed Jesus and fled, the "disciple whom Jesus loved" remained with his mother beside his cross as the dying Jesus entrusted to him his mother's care. John also says that this disciple, who had seen Roman soldiers hasten the death of other crucified men by breaking their legs, saw a soldier pierce Jesus' body with a spear. Later, when Mary Magdalene told him that

Jesus' body had disappeared from the grave, he and Peter ran to see what had happened. Luke says that Peter outran all the rest, and was the first to realize that Jesus had risen; but John says that Peter and the beloved disciple "both ran, but the other disciple outran Peter and reached the tomb first," so that *he* was the first who "saw and believed."[103] When the risen Jesus appeared to his disciples by Lake Gennesaret, the "disciple whom Jesus loved" was the first to recognize him and "said to Peter, 'It is the Lord!' "[104]

Although the author of this gospel may not have been one of "the twelve," he does acknowledge Peter's leadership—but with qualifications. John's final chapter, perhaps added later, tells how Jesus himself ordered Peter to care for his flock ("Feed my sheep").[105] But John adds that Jesus reserved for his "beloved disciple" a special, mysterious role that he refused to explain to Peter. When Peter saw that disciple and asked, "Lord, what about this man?" Jesus answered only, "If it is my will that he should remain until I come, what is that to you? Follow me!"[106] Such stories may imply that John's teaching, including the "farewell discourses" which Jesus addressed to the disciples, entrusting "the beloved disciple" to write them down, is superior to Peter's. Such stories suggest rivalry—but not necessarily opposition— between the Peter Christians and those whom John assumes to be his audience, the so-called Johannine Christians, who regard "the disciple whom Jesus loved" as their spiritual mentor.

Such stories, and the differences they show among various leaders and groups, involve more than power struggles: they involve the substance of Christian faith. As the stories themselves show, at stake is the central question Who is Jesus, and what is the "gospel" (good news) about him? Not surprisingly, each group characterizes its own patron apostle as the one who best understands "the gospel." So, for example, even the "gnostic" Gospel of Mary, like many other gospels, tells how its primary apostle—in this case, Mary Magdalene—received direct revelation from "the Lord," and claims that Jesus authorized her to teach.[107]

What John writes about Peter and "the beloved disciple" suggests that while John accepted the teaching associated with Peter, and even wrote his own gospel "so that you might believe that Jesus is the messiah, the son of God,"[108] his own teaching went further. So, while he agrees with Peter—and Mark—that Jesus is God's messiah, John goes further, and also insists that Jesus is actually *"Lord and God."*[109]

John must have known that this conviction branded him a radical among his fellow Jews—and even, apparently, among many of Jesus' followers. The scholar Louis Martyn suggests that John himself, along with those in his circle who shared his belief, had been accused of blasphemy for "making [Jesus] God" and forcibly expelled from their home synagogue.[110] In his gospel, John dramatizes this situation by turning a miracle story of Jesus healing a blind man into a parable for their own situation.[111] Speaking for himself and his fellow believers, John protested that their only crime was that God had opened their eyes to the truth, while the rest of the congregation remained blind. Thus in John's version, when Jesus met a man born blind, he "spat on the ground, made mud with the saliva, and spread it on the man's eyes, and said to him, 'Go, and wash in the pool of Siloam.' Then he went and washed and came back able to see."[112] But what the man had come to "see" was Jesus' divine power, which others denied; so, John says, "the Jews had already agreed that anyone who confessed Jesus to be the Messiah would be put out of the synagogue."[113] Although the man's parents—and thus, John implies, an older generation—did not dare to acknowledge Jesus' power because, he says, they were afraid that "the Jews" would expel them, the man whose eyes were opened defied the synagogue leaders by confessing faith in Jesus ("Lord, I believe") and worshiping him.[114]

Thus John's account implicitly places Jesus—and his power to heal and change lives—into his own time. By showing the man born blind facing expulsion from the synagogue, this story echoes John's own experience and that of his fellow believers. They, too, having been "born blind," now, thanks to Jesus, are able to "see"—but at the cost of rejection by their own people. So John's followers are relieved and grateful to hear Jesus' harsh, ironic words at the end of the story: "For judgment I came into this world, so that those who do not see may see; and so that those who do see may become blind."[115] Jesus says that he alone offers salvation: "All who came before me are thieves and robbers. . . . I am the door; whoever enters through me shall be saved."[116] Thus John's Jesus consoles his circle of disciples that, although hated "by the world," they alone belong to God.

Spurred by rejection but determined to make converts, John challenges his fellow Jews, including many who, like himself, follow Jesus. For John believes that those who regard Jesus merely as a prophet, or a rabbi, or even the future king of Israel, while not wrong, nevertheless are blind to his full "glory." John himself proclaims a more radical vision—one that finally alienates him from other Jews, and even from other Jewish followers of Jesus. Not only is Jesus Israel's future king, and so messiah and son of God, but, John declares, he is "greater than Moses" and older than Abraham. When he pictures Jesus declaring to a hostile crowd that "before Abraham was, *I am*,"[117] John expects his readers to hear Jesus claiming for himself the divine name that God revealed to Moses ("tell them that *I am* has sent you");[118] thus Jesus is nothing less than God himself, manifest in human form.

John warns those who doubt him that Jesus, acting as divine judge, will condemn those who reject this "good news," even if they constitute the main body of the Jewish people, rather than the handful of the faithful who alone see the truth and proclaim it to a hostile and unbelieving world. According to John, "the Jews" regard Jesus himself (and thus his followers) as insane or demon-possessed. John warns that, just as they wanted to kill Jesus for "making himself God," they will hate and want to kill his followers for believing such blasphemy: "Whoever kills you will think he is doing service to God."[119] But John assures Jesus' followers that God judges very differently: "Whoever believes in him [Jesus] is not condemned; but whoever does not believe is condemned already, because he has not believed in the name of the only begotten Son of God."[120] For John, Jesus has become more than the messenger of the kingdom—and even more than its future king: Jesus *himself* has become the message.

How could anyone who heard John's message—or that of Mark, Thomas, or any of the others, for that matter—decide what to believe? Various Christian groups validated their teaching by declaring allegiance to a specific apostle or disciple and claiming him (and sometimes her, for some claim Mary as a disciple) as their spiritual founder. As early as 50 to 60 C.E., Paul had complained that members of different groups would say, for example, "I am from Paul," or "I am from Apollos,"[121] for those who wrote stories about various apostles—including John, as well as Peter, Matthew, Thomas, and Mary Magdalene—would often promote their groups' teachings by claiming that Jesus favored their patron apostle, so that, while John acknowledges Peter as a leader, he insists that "the beloved disciple" surpassed Peter in spiritual understanding. He is aware that other groups make similar claims for other disciples. He seems to know, for example, of Thomas Christians, who claim that *their* patron apostle, Thomas, understood more than Peter. Though John's gospel begins by seeming to agree with Thomas about God's presence in Jesus, by the end John tells three anecdotes about Thomas to show how wrong these Thomas Christians are.

John's gospel begins by recalling, as Thomas does, the opening of the first chapter of Genesis—saying that, since the beginning of time, divine light, "the light of all people," has shone forth:

> *In the beginning* [Gen. 1:1] was the word, and the word was with God, and the word was God . . . what came into being in him was life, and *the life was the light of all people.*"[122]

But John's next lines suggest that he intends not to complement but to *reject* Thomas's claim that we have direct access to God through the divine image within us, for John immediately adds—three times!—that the divine light did not penetrate the deep darkness into which the world has plunged. Though he agrees that, since the beginning of time, the divine light "shines into the darkness," he also declares that *"the darkness has not grasped it."*[123] (Here the Greek verb *katalambanein*, which means "to seize," has a double meaning, as does the English verb "to grasp"). Moreover, he says that, although the divine light had come into the world, "and the world was made through it, *the world did not recognize it."*[124] John then adds that even when that light "came unto its own, *its own*—God's people, Israel—*did not receive it."*[125] Thus, because that divine light was not available to those "in the world," finally "the word became flesh and dwelt among us"[126] in the form of Jesus of Nazareth, so that some people now may declare triumphantly, as John does, "we saw his glory [the Greek term translates the Hebrew *kabod*, which means "shining," or "radiance"], the glory as of the only begotten son of the Father."[127] Thus the invisible God became visible and tangible in a unique moment of revelation. A letter later attributed to John declares that "we have seen [him] with our eyes, and we have touched [him] with our hands!"[128]

But to anyone who claims, as Thomas does, that we are (or may become) like Jesus, John emphatically says *no*: Jesus is unique or, as John loves to call him, *monogenes*—*"only begotten"* or "one of a kind"[129]—for he insists that God has only *one* son, and he is different from you and me. Though John goes further than the other three New Testament evangelists in saying that Jesus is not only a man raised to exalted status ("messiah," "son of God," or "son of man") but God himself in human form, and though he presumably agrees that human beings are made in God's image, as Genesis 1:26 teaches, he argues that humankind has no innate capacity to know God. What John's gospel does—and has succeeded ever after in persuading the majority of Christians to do—is claim that only by believing in Jesus can we find divine truth.

Because this claim is John's primary concern, his Jesus does not offer ethical and apocalyptic teachings as he does in Mark, Matthew, and Luke; he delivers no "sermon on the mount," no parables teaching how to act, no predictions of the end of time. Instead, in John's gospel—and only in this gospel—Jesus continually proclaims his divine identity, speaking in what New Testament scholars call the "I am" sayings: "I am the way; I am the truth; I am the light; I am the vine; I am the water of life"— all metaphors for the divine source that alone fulfills our deepest needs. What John's Jesus *does* require of his disciples is that they believe: "You believe in God; believe also in me."[130] Then, speaking intimately to those who believe, he urges them to "love one another as I have loved you."[131] Jesus tells them that this strong sense of mutual support will sustain believers as together they face hatred and persecution from outsiders.[132]

Now we can see how John's message contrasts with that of Thomas. Thomas's Jesus directs each disciple to discover the light within ("within a person of light there is light");[133] but John's Jesus declares instead that "I am the light of the world" and that "whoever does not come to me walks in darkness."[134] In Thomas, Jesus reveals to the disciples that "you are from the kingdom, and to it you shall return" and teaches them to say for themselves that "we come from the light"; but John's Jesus speaks as the only one who comes "from above" and so has rightful priority over everyone else: *"You are from below; I am from above. . . . The one who comes from above is above all."*[135] Only Jesus is from God, and he alone offers access to God. John never tires of repeating that one must believe in Jesus, follow Jesus, obey Jesus, and confess him alone as God's *only* son. We are not his "twin," much less (even potentially) his equal; we must follow him, believe in him, and revere him as God in person: thus John's Jesus declares that *"you will die in your sins, unless you believe that I am he."*[136]

We are so different from Jesus, John says, that he is our only hope of salvation. Were Jesus like ourselves, he could not save and deliver a human race that is "dying in sin." What gives John hope is his conviction that Jesus descended into the world as an atonement sacrifice to save us from sin and from eternal damnation, and then rose—bodily—from the dead. As John tells it, the story of Jesus' baptism reaches its climax not, as in Mark, when Jesus announces the coming of God's kingdom, but when John the Baptist announces that Jesus has come: "Behold—the lamb of God, who takes away the sin of the world!"[137]

To draw near to God we must be "born again, of water and the spirit"[138]—reborn through faith in Jesus. The spiritual life received in baptism requires supernatural nourishment; so, John's Jesus declares,

> unless you eat the flesh of the Son of Man and drink his blood, you have no life in you. Those who eat my flesh and drink my blood have eternal life, and I will raise them up on the last day, for my flesh is true food, and my blood is true drink.[139]

Jesus offers access to eternal life, shared when those who believe join together to participate in the sacred meal of bread and wine that celebrates Jesus' death and resurrection.

Mark, Matthew, and Luke mention Thomas only as one of "the twelve." John singles him out as "the doubter"—the one who failed to understand who Jesus is, or what he is saying, and rejected the testimony of the other disciples. John then tells how the risen Jesus personally appeared to Thomas in order to rebuke him, and brought him to his knees. From this we might conclude, as most Christians have for nearly two millennia, that Thomas was a particularly obtuse and faithless disciple—though many of John's Christian contemporaries revered Thomas as an extraordinary apostle, entrusted with Jesus' "secret words." The scholar Gregory Riley suggests that John portrays Thomas this way for the practical—and polemical—purpose of deprecating Thomas Christians and their teaching.[140] According to John, Jesus praises those "who have not seen, and yet believed" without demanding proof, and rebukes Thomas as "faithless" because he seeks to verify the truth from his own experience.

John offers three anecdotes that impose upon Thomas the image—Doubting Thomas!—he will have ever afterward in the minds of most Christians. In the first, Thomas, hearing Jesus say that he is going toward Judaea to raise Lazarus from the dead, does not believe him, and "speaks the desperate words, 'Let us go, so that we may die with him.' "[141] Thus John pictures Thomas as one who listens to Jesus in disbelief, imagining that he is merely human, like everyone else.

In the second episode, Jesus, anticipating his death, urges his disciples to trust in God and in himself, and promises to "prepare a place for you," and to show them the way to God, since, as he says, "you know where I am going, and you know the way.' "[142] Thomas alone, of all the disciples, objects that he knows nothing of the kind: "Thomas said to him, '. . . We do not know where you are going. How can we know the way?' " In answer, John's Jesus proclaims to this ignorant and obtuse disciple what

I believe John wants to say to everyone who fails to understand how unique Jesus is: "Jesus said to [Thomas], 'I am the way, the truth, and the life; *no one comes to the Father, except through me.'* "[143]

In the third episode Jesus even returns after his death to rebuke Thomas. Luke specifies that, after the crucifixion, the risen Jesus appeared to "the eleven,"[144] and Matthew agrees that he appeared to "the eleven disciples"[145]—all but Judas Iscariot—and conferred the power of the holy spirit upon "the eleven." But John's account differs. John says instead that *"Thomas, called 'the twin' . . . was not with them when Jesus came."*[146]

According to John, the meeting Thomas missed was crucial; for after Jesus greeted the *ten* disciples with a blessing, he formally designated them his apostles: "As the Father has sent me, so I send you." Then he "breathed upon them" to convey the power of the holy spirit; and finally he delegated to them his authority to forgive sins, or to retain them.[147] The implication of the story is clear: Thomas, having missed this meeting, is not an apostle, has not received the holy spirit, and lacks the power to forgive sins, which the others received directly from the risen Christ. Furthermore, when they tell Thomas about their encounter with Jesus, he answers in the words that mark him forever—in John's characterization—as Doubting Thomas: "Unless I see the mark of the nails in his hands, and put my finger in the mark of the nails, and my hand in his side, *I will not believe.*" A week later, the risen Jesus reappears and, in this climactic scene, John's Jesus rebukes Thomas for lacking faith and tells him to believe: *"Do not be faithless, but believe."* Finally Thomas, overwhelmed, capitulates and stammers out the confession, "My Lord and my God!"[148]

For John, this scene is the coup de grâce: finally Thomas understands, and Jesus warns the rest of the chastened disciples: "Have you believed because you have seen? Blessed are those who have not seen, and yet believe."[149] Thus John warns all his readers that they *must* believe what they cannot verify for themselves—namely, the gospel message to which he declares himself a witness[150]—or face God's wrath. John may have felt some satisfaction writing this scene; for here he shows Thomas giving up his search for experiential truth—his "unbelief"—to confess what John sees as the truth of his gospel: the message would not be lost on Thomas Christians.

Addressing those who see Jesus differently, John urges his uncompromising conviction: belief in Jesus alone offers salvation. To those who heed, John promises great reward: forgiveness of sins, solidarity with God's people, and the power to overcome death. In place of Thomas's cryptic sayings, John offers a simple formula, revealed through the story of Jesus' life, death, and resurrection: "God loves you; believe, and be saved." John adds to his narrative scenes that Christians have loved and retold for millennia: the wedding at Cana; Nicodemus's nighttime encounter with Jesus; Jesus meeting a Samaritan woman at a well and asking her for water; Pilate asking his prisoner, "What is truth?"; the crucified Jesus telling his "beloved disciple" to care for his mother; the encounter with "Doubting Thomas," and Mary Magdalene mistaking the risen Jesus for the gardener.

John, of course, prevailed. Toward the end of the second century, as we shall see in the next chapter, the church leader Irenaeus, as well as certain Christians in Asia Minor and Rome, championed his gospel and declared that it bore the authority of "John the apostle, the son of Zebedee," whom Irenaeus, like most Christians after him, identified with "the beloved disciple."[151] From that time to the present, Christians threatened by persecution, or met with hostility or misunderstanding, often have found consolation in John's declaration that, although hated by "the world," they are uniquely loved by God. And, even apart from persecution, the boundaries John's gospel draws between "the world" and those whom Jesus calls "his own" have offered innumerable Christians a basis of group solidarity grounded in the assurance of salvation.

But the discovery of Thomas's gospel shows us that other early Christians held quite different understandings of "the gospel." For what John rejects as religiously inadequate—the conviction that the divine dwells as "light" within all beings—is much like the hidden "good news" that Thomas's gospel proclaims.[152] Many Christians today who read the Gospel of Thomas assume at first that it is simply wrong, and deservedly called heretical. Yet what Christians have disparagingly called gnostic and heretical sometimes turn out to be forms of Christian teaching that are merely unfamiliar to us—unfamiliar precisely because of the active and successful opposition of Christians such as John.

How, then, did John prevail? To answer this question, let us look at the challenges that confronted the first generations of his readers.

CHAPTER THREE

tototot

GOD'S WORD
OR HUMAN WORDS?

About a year after I had written *The Gnostic Gospels*, I was sitting at tea one brilliant October afternoon at the Zen Center in San Francisco, a guest of the Roshi, along with Brother David Steindl-Rast, a Benedictine monk. The Roshi, an American whose name is Richard Baker, told us how he, as a young man, had gone from Boston to Kyoto, where he entered a Buddhist monastery and became a disciple of the Zen master Shunryu Suzuki Roshi. "But"—he laughed—"had I known the Gospel of Thomas, I wouldn't have had to become a Buddhist!" Brother David, who that morning had offered to the Zen students a succinct and incisive exposition of the Apostles' Creed, shook his head. Thomas and some other unorthodox gospels, he acknowledged, may be Christian mystical writings, but, he insisted, they are essentially no different from what the church offers: "There's nothing in those texts that you can't find in the writings of the great mystics of the church, like Saint Teresa, or Saint John of the Cross."

I said that I did not agree. In the first place, Teresa of Avila and John of the Cross—to say nothing of Jacob Boehme, the German mystic of the seventeenth century, and others like him, who were condemned and excommunicated as heretics—were intensely aware that whatever "revelations" they confided to their monastic superiors would have to conform—or seem to conform—to orthodox teaching. Christian mystics, like their Jewish and Muslim counterparts, have always been careful not to identify themselves with God. But the Gospel of Thomas teaches that recognizing one's affinity with God is the key to the kingdom of God. The remarkable modern scholar Theodor Gaster, the thirteenth son of the chief rabbi of London, observed that Jewish mystics are careful to speak of *relationship* with God but not of *identification:* "The Jewish mystic can say, with Martin Buber, 'I *and* Thou,' but can never say 'I *am* Thou,' which is permissible in Hindi religious teaching, for example, as in the phrase, *tat thvam asi* [literally, "Thou art *that*"]."[1]

Orthodox Jews and Christians, of course, have never wholly denied affinity between God and ourselves. But their leaders have tended to discourage or, at least, to circumscribe the process through which people may seek God on their own. This may be why some people raised as Christians and Jews today are looking elsewhere to supplement what they have not found in Western tradition. Even Father Thomas Keating, the former abbot of St. Joseph's Abbey in Spencer, Massachusetts, who has been a Cistercian monk for over fifty years, has sought through dialogue with the Buddhist and other wisdom traditions, as well as with contemporary science, to deepen the ancient practice he calls Centering Prayer. Fr. Keating finds that certain elements of Buddhist meditative practice complement Christian tradition by offering other experiential ways to discover divine truth. Thomas Merton, the famous monk who wrote the bestseller of the 1940s *The Seven Storey Mountain*, a Trappist like Keating, had similarly investigated Buddhist tradition. Thus even some devoted Christians have found that the impulse to seek God overflows the banks of a single tradition.

But as we have seen, within a century of Jesus' death, some of his most loyal followers had determined to exclude a wide range of *Christian* sources, to say nothing of borrowing from other religious traditions, although, as we have also seen, this often happened. But why, and in what circumstances, did these early church leaders believe that this was necessary for the movement to survive? And why did those who proclaimed Jesus the "only begotten son of God," as the Gospel of John declares, dominate later tradition, while other Christian visions, like that of Thomas, which encourages disciples to recognize themselves, as well as Jesus, as "children of God," were suppressed?

Traditionally, Christian theologians have declared that "the Holy Spirit guides the church into all truth"—a statement often taken to mean that what has survived must be right. Some historians of religion have rationalized this conviction by implying that in Christian history, as in the history of science, weak, false ideas die off early, while the strong and valid ones survive. The late Raymond Brown, a prominent New Testament scholar and Roman Catholic Sulpician priest, stated this perspective baldly: What orthodox Christians rejected was only "the rubbish of the second century"—and, he added, "it's still rubbish."[2] But such polemics tell us nothing about how and why early church leaders laid down the fundamental principles of Christian teaching. To understand what happened we need to look at the specific challenges—and dangers—that confronted believers during the critical years around 100 to 200 C.E., and how those who became the architects of Christian tradition dealt with these challenges.

The African convert Tertullian, living in the port city of Carthage in North Africa about eighty years after the Gospels of John and Thomas were written, around the year 190 (or, as Tertullian and his contemporaries might have said, during the reign of Emperor Commodus), acknowledged that the Christian movement was attracting crowds of new members—and that outsiders were alarmed:

> The outcry is that the State is filled with Christians—that they are in the fields, in the cities, in the islands; and [outsiders] lament, as if for some calamity, that both men and women, of every age and condition, even high rank, are going over to profess Christian faith.[3]

Tertullian ridiculed the non-Christian majority for their wild suspicions and denounced the magistrates for believing them:

> [We are called] monsters of evil, and accused of practicing a sacred ritual in which we kill a little child and eat it; in which, after the feast, we practice incest, while the dogs, our pimps, overturn the lights and give us the shameless darkness to gratify our lusts. *This is what people constantly*

charge, yet you take no trouble to find out the truth. . . .
Well, *you think the Christian is capable of every crime—an enemy of
the gods, of the emperor, of the laws, of good morals, of all nature.*[4]

Tertullian was distressed that throughout the empire, from his
native city in Africa to Italy, Spain, Egypt, and Asia Minor, and
in the provinces from Germany to Gaul, Christians had become
targets of sporadic outbreaks of violence. Roman magistrates
often ignored these incidents and sometimes participated in
them. In the city of Smyrna on the coast of Asia Minor, for example, crowds shouting "Get the atheists!" lynched the convert
Germanicus and demanded—successfully—that the authorities
arrest and immediately kill Polycarp, a prominent bishop.[5]

What outsiders saw depended considerably on which Christian groups they happened to encounter. Pliny, governor of
Bithynia, in modern Turkey, trying to prevent groups from shel-
tering subversives, ordered his soldiers to arrest people accused
as Christians. To gather information, his soldiers tortured two
Christian women, both slaves, who revealed that members of
this peculiar cult "met regularly before dawn on a certain day to
sing a hymn to Christ as to a god." Though it had been rumored
that they were eating human flesh and blood, Pliny found that
they were actually eating only "ordinary, harmless food." He reported to the emperor Trajan that, although he found no evidence of actual crime, "I ordered them to be taken away and
executed; for, whatever they admit to, I am convinced that their
stubbornness and unshakable obstinacy should not go unpun-
ished."[6] But twenty years later in Rome, Rusticus, the city prefect, interrogated a group of five Christians who looked to him

less like members of a cult than like a philosophy seminar. Justin Martyr the philosopher, arraigned along with his students, admitted to the prefect that he met with like-minded believers in his Roman apartment "above the baths of Timothy" to discuss "Christian philosophy."[7] Nevertheless Rusticus, like Pliny, suspected treason. When Justin and his pupils refused his order to sacrifice to the gods, he had them beaten, then beheaded.

Thirty years after Justin's death, another philosopher, named Celsus, who detested Christians, wrote a book called *The True Word*, which exposed their movement and accused some of them of acting like wild-eyed devotees of foreign gods such as Attis and Cybele, possessed by spirits. Others, Celsus charged, practiced incantations and spells, like magicians; still others followed what many Greeks and Romans saw as the barbaric, Oriental customs of the Jews. Celsus reported, too, that on large estates throughout the countryside Christian woolworkers, cobblers, and washerwomen, people who, he said, "ordinarily are afraid to speak in the presence of their superiors," nevertheless gathered the gullible—slaves, children, and "stupid women"—from the great houses into their workshops to hear how Jesus worked miracles and, after he died, rose from the grave.[8] Among respectable citizens, Christians aroused the same suspicions of violence, promiscuity, and political extremism with which secretive cults are still regarded, especially by those who fear that their friends or relatives may be lured into them.

Despite the diverse forms of early Christianity—and perhaps because of them—the movement spread rapidly, so that by the end of the second century Christian groups were proliferating throughout the empire, despite attempts to stop them. Tertul-

lian boasted to outsiders that "the more we are mown down by
you, the more we multiply; the blood of Christians is seed!"[9] De-
fiant rhetoric, however, could not solve the problem that he and
other Christian leaders faced: How could they strengthen and
unify this enormously diverse and widespread movement, so it
could survive its enemies?

Tertullian's younger contemporary Irenaeus, often identified
as bishop of Lyons, himself had experienced the hostility Tertullian was talking about, first in his native town of Smyrna
(Izmir, in today's Turkey) and then in the rough provincial town
of Lyons, in Gaul (now France). Irenaeus also witnessed the frac-
tiousness that divided Christian groups. As a boy he had lived
in the household of his teacher Polycarp, the venerable bishop
of Smyrna, whom even his enemies called the teacher of Asia
Minor.[10] Although he knew that they were scattered in many
small groups throughout the world, Irenaeus shared Polycarp's
hope that Christians everywhere would come to see themselves
as members of a single church they called catholic, which means
"universal."[11] To unify this worldwide community, Polycarp urged
its members to reject all deviants. According to Irenaeus, Polycarp liked to tell how his own mentor, "John, the disciple of the
Lord"—the same person whom tradition reveres as the author
of the Gospel of John—once went to the public baths in Ephesus, but, seeing Cerinthus, whom he regarded as a heretic, John
"ran out of the bath house without bathing, exclaiming, 'Let
us flee, lest the bath house fall down; because Cerinthus, the
enemy of the truth, is inside.'" When Irenaeus repeated this
story, he added another to show how Polycarp himself treated
heretics. When the influential but controversial Christian teacher
Marcion confronted the bishop and asked him, "Do you rec-

ognize me?" Polycarp replied, "Yes, I recognize you—firstborn of Satan!"[12]

Irenaeus says that he tells these stories to show "the horror that the apostles and their disciples had against even speaking with those who corrupt the truth."[13] But his stories also show what troubled Irenaeus: that even two generations after the author of the Gospel of John qualified the claims of Peter Christians and confronted Thomas Christians, the movement remained contentious and divided. Polycarp himself denounced people who, he charged, "bear the [Christian] name with evil deceit"[14] because what they teach often differs from what he had learned from his own teachers. Irenaeus, in turn, believed that he practiced true Christianity, for he could link himself directly to the time of Jesus through Polycarp, who personally had heard Jesus' teaching from John himself, "the disciple of the Lord."[15] Convinced that this disciple wrote the Gospel of John, Irenaeus was among the first to champion this gospel and link it forever to Mark, Matthew, and Luke. His contemporary Tatian, a brilliant Syrian student of Justin Martyr the philosopher, killed by Rusticus, took a different approach: he tried to unify the various gospels by rewriting all of them into a single text.[16] Irenaeus left the texts intact but declared that only Matthew, Mark, Luke, and John collectively—and only these gospels exclusively—constitute the whole gospel, which he called the "four formed gospel."[17] Only these four gospels, Irenaeus believed, were written by eyewitnesses to events through which God has sent salvation to humankind.[18] This four gospel canon was to become a powerful weapon in Irenaeus's campaign to unify and consolidate the Christian movement during his lifetime, and it has remained a basis of orthodox teaching ever since.

While he supervised and taught his fellow believers in Smyrna, Polycarp sent one of his associates, Pothinus, to organize and unify a group of Greek-speaking Christians from the same region who had settled in the western hinterlands of Celtic Gaul. Later he sent his protégé, Irenaeus, then sixteen or seventeen years old, to work with Pothinus. In the winter of 167, however, when public hostility against Christians broke out in Smyrna, Roman police arrested Polycarp, whom they found hiding in a friend's country estate. Accused of atheism, and ordered by the governor to swear an oath to the emperor's *genius* (the spirit of his family), to curse Christ, and to say "Away with the atheists" (the Christians), Polycarp refused. Marched into the public stadium, the eighty-six-year-old bishop shook his fist at the hostile, noisy crowd and defiantly shouted, "Away with the atheists!" He was then stripped naked, bound to a stake, and burned alive.[19] Irenaeus, visiting in Rome at the time, says that on that very afternoon, of February 23, 167 c.e., he heard a voice "like a trumpet call" revealing to him what was happening to his beloved teacher. From accounts of eyewitnesses, he (or another of Polycarp's students) later wrote a moving report of his teacher's arrest, interrogation, and death.

Ten years later Irenaeus, perhaps still in his twenties, witnessed mob violence against Christians at first hand in Lyons, where he lived, and in the town of Vienne, some thirty miles away. Public officials had banned Christians, as polluted persons, from entering the baths and markets and, finally, from all public places protected by the city's gods. Then, when the provincial governor was away from the city, "the mob broke loose. Christians were hounded and attacked openly. They were treated as public enemies, assaulted, beaten, and stoned."[20] Bishop Pothi-

nus, now in his nineties, was arrested and tortured, along with between thirty and fifty of the most outspoken members of his congregation. Many were taken to prison and strangled. Ten Christians changed their minds and recanted but were not released. Those who survived and still confessed to being Christians were sentenced to be tortured in public and torn apart by wild animals. When the governor returned and heard that some of the prisoners were Roman citizens, he wrote to Marcus Aurelius, the so-called philosopher emperor, to ask whether these should die in a public spectacle in the arena like the rest or be granted the citizens' usual privilege of a quicker, more private death—for example, by beheading.

We do not know what the emperor replied; but meanwhile those terrified Christians who managed to escape arrest marveled at how God's power energized the confessors. At their trial, for example, the young nobleman Vettius Epagathus dared to defend them before a hostile, shouting crowd. When the magistrate, apparently irritated by his objections, turned to him and asked, "Are you one of them too?" the sympathizer who wrote their story says that the holy spirit inspired him to say yes, and so to die with them.[21] God's spirit filled the least of them as well: some said that it was Christ himself who suffered in the slave girl Blandina, when she astonished everyone by withstanding the most agonizing torture; and others told how Christ triumphed in the suffering of the slave named Sanctus, and inspired Bishop Pothinus's unwavering courage until he expired. Many testified that they had experienced the power of the holy spirit as they prayed together in the dark, stinking prison of Lyons.

But when the imprisoned confessors heard from their visitors that in Rome *other* "spirit filled" Christians were being persecuted—and not by Roman magistrates but, worse, by their fellow Christians—they decided to intervene. Claiming the special authority that Christians accorded those who had given up their lives for Christ, they wrote a letter to the bishop of Rome, urging him to deal peaceably with those under attack, who had joined a revival movement called "the new prophecy." The prisoners asked Irenaeus, who had somehow escaped arrest, to travel to Rome to deliver their letter, and he agreed.

Irenaeus does not tell us his own attitude toward the new prophecy, but he probably knew that this movement of charismatic Christians had arisen about ten years before in rural towns of his native Asia Minor (present-day Turkey), when the prophets Montanus, Maximilla, and Priscilla, popularly called "the three," began traveling from one rural church to another, claiming to communicate directly with the holy spirit. Wherever they went, the three shared their visions, spoke in ecstasy, and urged others to fast and pray so that they too could receive visions and revelations. From Asia Minor the movement swept through churches all across the empire, to Africa, Rome, and Greece, and even to remote provinces like Gaul, arousing enthusiasm—and opposition.

Apollinarius, who became bishop of the Asian town of Hierapolis in 171 c.e., says that when he went to Ancyra (contemporary Ankara, in Turkey) "and saw that the church in that place was torn in two by this new movement," he opposed it, declaring that "it is not *prophecy,* as they call it, but, as I shall show, *false prophecy.*"[22] Such opponents accused Montanus, Maximilla, and Priscilla of being opportunists, or even demon-possessed. In one town a Christian named Zotimus interrupted Maximilla while she was prophesying and tried to exorcise her, ordering her "demons" to leave, until her followers seized him and dragged him outside the church. Maximilla had received outpourings of the spirit and had left her husband to devote herself to prophecy. Speaking in an ecstatic trance, she declared, "Do not listen to me, but to Christ. . . . I am compelled, whether willing or not, to come to know God's *gnosis*."[23] Priscilla claimed that Christ had appeared to her in female form. Opponents accused both Maximilla and Priscilla of breaking their marriage vows, wearing expensive clothes, and making money by deceiving gullible people. After a group of bishops in Turkey finally excommunicated her, Maximilla protested: "I am driven away like the wolf from the sheep. I am no wolf; I am word, and spirit, and power!"[24]

When Irenaeus arrived in Rome, he found on every side groups and factions that challenged his own understanding of the gospel. The letter he brought may have helped persuade Bishop Eleutherus to refrain from censuring the new prophecy, but the movement was dividing Christians throughout Asia Minor as well as Rome. While many attacked its leaders as liars and frauds, others defended it—and those on both sides drew the Gospel of John into the controversy. Some members of the new prophecy claimed that the spirit's presence among them fulfilled what Jesus promised in John's gospel: "I will send you the advocate [*paraclete*], the spirit of truth, . . . [who] will guide you into all truth."[25] Angered by such argument, Gaius, a Christian leader in Rome, charged that the Gospel of John, along with that other controversial book of "spiritual prophecy," the Revelation, was written not by "John, the disciple of the Lord," but by his worst enemy, Cerinthus—the man whom Polycarp said John had personally denounced as a heretic.[26] Not long afterward, however, Tertullian, already famous as a champion of orthodoxy, himself joined the new prophecy and defended its members as genuinely spirit-filled Christians. Although to this day Tertullian stands among the "fathers of the church," at the end of his life he turned against what, at this point, he now began to call "the church of a bunch of bishops."[27]

When Irenaeus met in Rome a childhood friend from Smyrna named Florinus, who like himself as a young man had studied with Polycarp, he was shocked to learn that his friend now had joined a group headed by Valentinus and Ptolemy—sophisticated theologians who, nevertheless, like the new prophets, often relied on dreams and revelations.[28] Although they called themselves spiritual Christians, Irenaeus regarded them as dangerously deviant. Hoping to persuade his friend to reconsider, Irenaeus wrote a letter to warn him that "these views, Florinus, to put it mildly, are not sound; are not consonant with the church, and involve their devotees in the worst impiety, even heresy."[29] Irenaeus was distressed to learn that an increasing number of educated Christians were moving in the same direction.

When he returned from Rome to Gaul, Irenaeus found his own community devastated; some thirty people had been brutally tortured and killed in the public arena on a day set aside to entertain the townspeople with this spectacle. With Bishop Pothinus dead, the remaining members of his group now looked to Irenaeus for leadership. Aware of the danger, he nevertheless agreed, determined to unify the survivors. But he saw that members of his own "flock" were splintered into various, often fractious groups—all of them claiming to be inspired by the holy spirit.

How could he sort out these conflicting claims and impose some kind of order? The task was enormous and perplexing. Irenaeus believed, certainly, that the holy spirit had initiated the Christian movement. From the time it began, a hundred and fifty years earlier, both Jesus and his followers claimed to have experienced outpourings of the holy spirit—dreams, visions, stories, sayings, ecstatic speech—many communicated orally, many others written down—reflecting the vitality and diversity of the movement. The New Testament gospels abound in visions, dreams, and revelations, like the one that Mark says initiated Jesus' public activity:

In those days, Jesus came from Nazareth, and was baptized by John in the Jordan. And just as he was coming up out of the water, *he saw the heavens torn apart and the spirit descending like a dove upon him, and a voice came from heaven:* "You are my beloved son; with you I am well pleased."[30]

Luke adds to his version of this story an account of Jesus' birth, in which a vision precedes every event in the drama, from the moments the angel Gabriel appeared to the aging priest Zacharias and later to Mary, to the night when "an angel of the Lord" appeared to shepherds to tell them of Jesus' birth, terrifying them with a sudden radiance that lighted up the nighttime sky.[31]

But the visions and dreams that occurred during Jesus' life-time were overshadowed by those the gospels say happened after his death, when his grieving followers heard that "the Lord actually has risen and has appeared to Simon [Peter]!"[32] Each gospel indicates that Jesus' disciples received visions after his death, a time that Luke says was especially charged with super-natural power. For Luke, this outpouring of dreams and visions proved that God's spirit was present to Jesus' followers. This, he says, is what the prophet Joel had predicted:

In the last days it will be, God declares, that I will pour out my spirit upon all flesh, and your sons and your daugh-ters shall prophesy, and your young men shall see visions, and your old men shall dream dreams.[33]

Decades before Luke wrote, his mentor, Paul of Tarsus, then unknown to Jesus' disciples—or known to them all too well as an enemy and a spy—suddenly claimed that Jesus had person-ally appeared to him in a blazing light and chosen him as his special representative. Henceforth Paul, who had never met Jesus during his lifetime, called himself "an apostle of Jesus Christ" (*apostolos*, in Greek, means "representative") and claimed to rely on the spirit's direct guidance throughout his life.[34] Paul wrote to Christians in Corinth that he had been "caught up into Paradise," but said that what he had seen and heard there he could never tell, since these were "things that no mortal is allowed to speak."[35] Luke relates in the Acts of the Apostles, which he wrote as a sequel to the gospel, that even after the risen Jesus appeared personally to his astounded disciples and then ascended into heaven forty days later, the spirit continued to flood his followers with *charismata*—power to heal, to exorcise, to prophesy, even to raise the dead.

Even a hundred years or so after Luke wrote these things, members of the new prophecy loved to recall what the Gospel of John says Jesus promised to his followers: "The holy spirit will guide you into all truth" and enable you "to do greater works than I do."[36] Then, as now, many Christians believed that the author of that gospel also wrote the Revelation, which describes astonishing visions the author says he received "in the spirit," that is, in an ecstatic state. The author of Revelation, whose name was John, says that, while imprisoned on the island of Patmos "because of God's word and the witness to Jesus," he was "caught up into heaven" and beheld the Lord enthroned in glory above a heavenly sea, glittering like crystal, and heard angels intoning the secrets of "what is to come."[37] Unlike Paul, however, John *did* write down what he said he saw and heard in heaven, and this is why his book is called Revelation.

Without visions and revelations, then, the Christian movement would not have begun. But who can tell the holy spirit when to stop—or, as Irenaeus's contemporaries might have said, who can say whether the holy spirit *has* stopped? And when so many people—some of them rivals or even antagonists—all claim to be divinely inspired, who knows who has the spirit and who does not? These questions concerned Irenaeus—and concern many Christians today. Some ask now, as many did then, whether people living *after* the time of the apostles still receive direct revelation. A growing number of charismatic Christians today believe that they do, and some, unlike Irenaeus, believe that the spirit may say different things to different people. Those who call themselves Pentecostalists, for example, identify with the apostles Luke describes in the New Testament Acts of the Apostles. Luke tells how the apostles, at the feast of Pentecost, experienced God's spirit streaming down upon them "like tongues of fire" and filling them with power.[38] Those early Christians who joined the new prophecy no doubt agreed. One anonymous member of the movement objected to "those who want to restrict the power of the one Spirit to seasons and times" and declared that, on the contrary, "we recognize and honor not only new prophecies but new visions as well."[39]

Yet their opponents, including Gaius in Rome, argued that genuine visions and revelations had ended with the close of the apostolic age. Gaius urged his fellow believers to reject any revelation received after that time—from the visions in the Revelation to those of the new prophets. For, Gaius argued, since "the number of the prophets and apostles is [now] complete,"[40] no one who lived after the apostolic age could receive revelation directly from Jesus himself. As for Luke's story of the day of Pentecost, those who agreed with Gaius could point out that in that same opening scene in Acts, Jesus' disciples communed directly with the risen Christ for *only forty days*. Luke says that after forty days, "as they were looking on, he was lifted up, and a cloud took him out of their sight,"[41] forever ending direct communication between the risen Jesus and his disciples.

Irenaeus himself tried to forge a middle ground. Unlike Gaius, he refused to draw a sharp line between the apostolic age and the present. After all, he himself had received revelation—for example, on the day of Polycarp's death. He had heard, too, that Polycarp, while hiding from the police, had dreamed that his pillow caught fire and prophesied that "I am to be burnt alive."[42] Irenaeus also heard from the martyrs in his own town, as well as from other Christians, that such things still happen:

> We hear many brothers and sisters in the church who have prophetic gifts, speaking through the spirit in all kinds of tongues, and bringing things hidden from human beings into clarity, and revealing the mysteries of God.[43]

So Irenaeus challenged those who suggested that miracle stories in the gospels were not to be taken literally, or that miracles no longer happen:

> Those who are truly his disciples actually do drive out demons. . . . Others foresee things that will happen; they see visions and speak prophecies . . . others, still, heal the sick by laying their hands upon them, and they are completely healthy. . . .
>
> Yes, and furthermore, as I have said, even the dead have been raised up, and they have remained alive among us for many years. What more should I say? It is not possible to tell how many gifts which the church throughout the world has received in the name of Jesus Christ, and uses every day to benefit the nations, neither deceiving anyone, nor taking any money.[44]

These miracles attracted crowds of newcomers to Christian groups, despite the danger. Those who receive healing, Irenaeus added, "often believe and join the church."[45]

Although Irenaeus stopped short of defending Maximilla,

Montanus, and Priscilla, or even mentioning the new prophets by name—if, indeed, he knew their names—he criticized their opponents for wrongly "disregarding both the gospel [of John] and the spirit of prophecy." He reminded his contemporaries that Paul, too, not only received visions and spoke prophecies but also "recognized men and women prophesying in the churches."[46]

But the immediate problem Irenaeus confronted in Lyons was not a lack of spiritual revelation but an overwhelming surplus. Perhaps he refrained from criticizing the new prophets because he thought the things they said when they spoke "in the spirit" did not deviate that much from the tradition he accepted. But *other* would-be prophets said and did things he thought were completely wrong, and Irenaeus judged them to be schismatics and frauds. The problem was how to discriminate: "How," he asked, "can we tell the difference between the word of God and mere human words?"[47]

What especially troubled Irenaeus was that "even in our own district of the Rhone valley," a prophet named Marcus was causing a stir among believers; he had attracted from Irenaeus's congregation

> a great number of men and quite a few women . . . whom he [had] persuaded to join him, as one who possesses the greatest understanding and maturity, and who has received the highest power from the invisible and ineffable regions above.[48]

Although his account is hostile, and accuses Marcus of being an agent of Satan, Irenaeus offers a detailed picture of what this prophet did. Marcus not only received visions and spoke in prophecy himself but also encouraged others to do so. When someone asked Marcus to invoke the power of the spirit, Marcus would place his hands upon the person's head and offer prayer that echoed Jesus' words from the Gospel of Matthew ("Do not despise the little ones, for, I tell you, their angels continually see the face of my Father in heaven").[49] Marcus prayed for each initiate that "you may receive grace, since the Father of all sees your angel standing before him." Then he placed his hands upon the person's head and said, "Behold, grace has descended upon you; open your mouth, and prophesy." Then, Irenaeus says, the candidate would protest, having been instructed to do so, that "I have not at any time prophesied, nor do I know how to prophesy," in order to acknowledge that prophecy has nothing to do with natural human capacity but only with the gift of divine grace. Finally Marcus again would encourage the initiate to speak prophecy—often, Irenaeus says, a "foolish woman"—and at that point, he says indignantly,

> she, then, puffed up with vanity and elated by these words, and enormously excited in soul by expecting that she herself is about to prophesy, her heart beating wildly, reaches the necessary pitch of audacity, and, foolishly as well as brazenly, utters whatever nonsense happens to occur to her, such as one might expect from someone heated up by an empty spirit.[50]

Having received the spirit through this initiation, each member of Marcus's circle believed that he or she shared "the gift of prophecy." When they would gather to celebrate the sacred meal, the eucharist, Irenaeus says that "all of them [were] accustomed to cast lots." Thus they followed an ancient Israelite practice, which, as Luke says in Acts, Christians revived, of throwing lots in order to invite the holy spirit to show, by the way the lots fell, whom the spirit chose to offer that day's prophecy.[51]

As Irenaeus tells it—perhaps adding details for the sake of sensation—Marcus claimed that divine truth had revealed itself to him naked, "in feminine form, having descended upon him from invisible and ineffable space, for the world could not have borne [the truth] coming in masculine form."[52] According to Irenaeus, Marcus said that she revealed herself through letters and numbers, each part of her body adorned with one of the twenty-four letters of the Greek alphabet; and she spoke the mystical name "Christ Jesus."[53] The letters and numbers in which Marcus received his vision reflected Jewish traditions known to followers of his spiritual teacher, Valentinus, who claimed to be initiated into Paul's secret wisdom teaching. Similar traditions would flower, more than a thousand years later, among mystically inclined Jewish groups, who would call them *kabbalah*.

Although the Hebrew term simply means "tradition," *kabbalah* radically transforms tradition. The late Gershom Scholem, professor of Jewish mysticism at the Hebrew University of Jerusalem, far more sympathetic to Marcus than Irenaeus was, explained that those who take the path of *kabbalah* seek to know God "not through dogmatic theology but through living experience and intuition."[54] Like other Jews, kabbalists interpret the Scriptures; but in their hands the Scriptures become the language of spiritual exploration. Like kabbalists more than a thousand years later, Marcus asked, How can we speak of what is ineffable? How can the invisible, incomprehensible God become manifest? Marcus's vision suggests that the whole alphabet—all of human speech—can become a mystical form of divine truth—a conviction that many kabbalists would share.

Like many others, Marcus was fascinated with Genesis, as he wondered what happened "in the beginning"—and even *before* the beginning—of the universe. And like the authors of Thomas and John, Marcus interpreted Genesis 1, and suggested that "when first the unbegotten, inconceivable father, who is neither male nor female, willed to bring forth . . . he opened his mouth and spoke the word" (*logos*).[55] Marcus explained that, as he envisioned this process, each separate letter that God spoke at first recognized neither its own nature nor that of the others, for "while every one of them is part of the whole, each one imagines its own sound to be the whole name" of the divine being. Yet, Marcus continued, "the restoration of all things will take place" only when this illusion of separateness is overcome, and "all these [elements], mingling into one sound, shall join unanimously" in the same song of praise.[56] For the universe itself came forth from "the glory of that sound of praise." Marcus believed that this is something everyone knows intuitively, and acknowledges from the first cry a newborn utters emerging from the womb to those moments of anguish when a person moans or cries out "in difficulty and distress . . . saying 'oh.' "[57] Such sounds, Marcus said, echo the divine name, which, he believed, people instinctively—even unconsciously—utter in the form of spontaneous prayer for divine help. And when people join their voices together in worship to chant "Amen" (Hebrew for "May it be so"), their unanimous voice anticipates how all that exists finally shall be restored into a single, harmonious whole.

Irenaeus says that he tried hard, at a friend's request, to investigate Marcus's teaching in order to expose him as an interloper and a fraud. For by attracting disciples, performing initiations, and offering special teachings to "spiritual" Christians, Marcus's activity threatened Irenaeus's effort to unify all Christians in the area into a homogenous church. Irenaeus charged that Marcus was a magician, "the herald of Antichrist"—a man whose made-up visions and pretense to spiritual power masked his true identity as Satan's own apostle.[58] He ridiculed Marcus's claims to investigate "the deep things of God" and mocked him for urging initiates to seek revelations of their own:

> While they say such things as these about the creation, every one of them generates something new every day, according to his ability; for no one is considered "mature" [or "initiated"] among them who does not develop some enormous lies.[59]

Irenaeus expresses dismay that many other teachers, too, within Christian communities, "introduce an indescribable number of secret and illegitimate writings, which they themselves have forged, to bewilder the minds of foolish people, who are ignorant of the true scriptures."[60] He quotes some of their writings, including part of a well-known and influential text called the Secret Book of John (discovered among the so-called gnostic gospels at Nag Hammadi in 1945), and he refers to many others, including a Gospel of Truth (perhaps the one discovered at Nag

Hammadi), which he attributes to Marcus's teacher, Valentinus, and even a Gospel of Judas. Irenaeus decided that stemming this flood of "secret writings" would be an essential first step toward limiting the proliferation of "revelations" that he suspected of being only delusional or, worse, demonically inspired.[61] Yet the discoveries at Nag Hammadi show how widespread was the attempt "to seek God"—not only among those who wrote such "secret writings" but among the many more who read, copied, and revered them, including the Egyptian monks who treasured them in their monastery library even two hundred years after Irenaeus had denounced them. But in 367 C.E., Athanasius, the zealous bishop of Alexandria—an admirer of Irenaeus—issued an Easter letter in which he demanded that Egyptian monks destroy all such writings, except for those he specifically listed as "acceptable," even "canonical"—a list that constitutes virtually all of our present "New Testament."[62] But someone—perhaps monks at the monastery of St. Pachomius—gathered dozens of the books Athanasius wanted to burn, removed them from the monastery library, sealed them in a heavy, six-foot jar, and intending to hide them, buried them on a nearby hillside near Nag Hammadi. There an Egyptian villager named Muhammad 'Alī stumbled upon them sixteen hundred years later.

Now that we can read for ourselves some of the writings that Irenaeus detested and Athanasius banned, we can see that many of them express the hope of receiving revelation, and encourage "those who seek for God." The author of the Secret Book of James, for example, *reinterprets* the opening scene we noted from the New Testament Acts, in which Luke tells how Jesus ascended into heaven and departed. The Secret Book, apparently written as a *sequel* to that scene, opens as James, Jesus' brother, offers to reveal in this book what happened *after* Jesus "departed from us while we gazed after him."[63] After that, he says,

> the twelve disciples were all sitting together and recalling what the Savior had said to each one of them, either secretly or openly, and putting it into books, and I was writing what is in my book.[64]

But the Secret Book says that Jesus astonished his disciples by suddenly coming back—a year and a half after he had departed—and explained that he had not actually removed himself from his disciples:

> Lo, the Savior appeared. . . . And *five hundred and fifty days* since he had risen from the dead, we said to him, *"Have you departed and removed yourself from us?"* But Jesus said, *"No; but I go to the place whence I came. If you wish to come with me, come!"*[65]

According to the Secret Book, Jesus then invited James and Peter to travel with him to heaven, perhaps in the kind of ecstatic trance that John of Patmos said he experienced before he wrote the book of Revelation. First Jesus separated them from the others and privately explained that they could join him not only after death but also here and now, by becoming "full of the spirit."[66] But instead of urging his disciples simply to *follow* him, here Jesus encourages them to *surpass* him. He explains that those who suffer and overcome the fear of death may "become better than I; make yourselves like the son of the Holy Spirit! Be zealous, and if possible, arrive [in heaven] even before I do."[67] As the Secret Book concludes, James tells how

> Peter and I gave thanks, and sent our hearts upward toward heaven. We heard with our ears, and saw with our eyes, the noise of war, trumpets blaring and a great turmoil. And when we had passed beyond that place, we sent our minds farther upwards, and saw with our eyes and heard with our ears . . . angels rejoicing, as we, too, rejoiced.[68]

Many other Christians who sought revelation—and may even have hoped to ascend into heaven during their lifetime—took Paul, naturally enough, as their patron apostle. The author of the Prayer of the Apostle Paul, discovered at Nag Hammadi, is one of many to recall what Paul wrote in his letter to Christians in Corinth about his own "visions and revelations of the Lord," especially the famous episode in which Paul says he was

> caught up into the third heaven—whether in the body or out of the body, I do not know; God knows. . . . I heard things that are not to be spoken, that no mortal is allowed to speak.[69]

The author of the Prayer of the Apostle Paul, then, takes Paul as the paradigm of "those who seek for God" and articulates the longing to enter into God's presence, as Paul had:

My redeemer, redeem me, for I am yours, one who has come forth from you. You are my mind; bring me forth. You are my treasure; open to me. You are my fulfillment; join me to you![70]

Finally, echoing what Paul writes in his first letter to the Corinthians, the prayer concludes, "Grant what no angel's eye has seen and what no ruling power's ear has heard, and what has not entered into the human heart . . . since I have faith and hope."[71]

Those who wrote, translated, and carefully copied works such as the Secret Book of James and the Prayer of the Apostle Paul may have known about techniques that certain Jewish groups used to induce a state of ecstasy and invoke visions. For example, one group of Jewish ascetics living in Egypt at the time of Jesus, called the Therapeutae, practiced a rigorous regimen of prayer, celibacy, fasting, and singing to prepare themselves to receive "the vision of God." Some of the Dead Sea Scrolls also offer prayers and rituals apparently intended to help the devout enter God's presence and join in worship with angels.[72]

We do not know precisely what was meant by "the vision of God." Different people probably conceived it differently. Some scholars take this phrase to mean that such people sought to experience God's presence through ecstatic trance.[73] Paul's account of his own ascent into Paradise suggests that this happened to him, although, as we noted, he claims that his vision occurred spontaneously and admits that "whether in the body or out of the body, I do not know; God knows."[74] Other scholars, however, point out that those who say they are seeking a vision of God may be referring to what happens in devotional practices and worship.[75] For to this day many Jews and Christians use mystical language in worship services every week—or even every day—at a culminating moment understood to unite the human congregation with the angels, as they join in singing what the prophet Isaiah says angels sing in heaven: "Holy, holy, holy; Lord God almighty; heaven and earth are full of your glory." Isaiah says that he heard this song when he himself received a vision and was taken into God's presence.[76]

Scholars of Jewish history and literature are also investigating an enormous wealth of mystical literature that flourished for about a thousand years preceding *kabbalah*. Some of these so-called *hekalot* texts focus upon the figure of Enoch, who, according to Genesis, "walked with God" and, without dying, was taken up into God's presence.[77] Even before the first century B.C.E., Enoch had become a paradigm for those seeking access to heavenly wisdom.[78] Other groups of Jews were devoted to the so-called Merkabah (chariot) literature, which thrived from the second century through the sixth. These writings emerged from Jewish teachers and their disciples who tried to act upon hints they found in the prophet Ezekiel's marvelous vision of God enthroned upon a chariot shining like fire, borne by winged cherubim, and praised by the angelic host.[79]

Some of those who described visions like the ones found in the Secret Book of James seem to imply that they themselves, like the prophets Isaiah and Ezekiel, received such visions. Some of the books discovered at Nag Hammadi offer specific techniques for invoking revelations; others suggest that such techniques did not always work. The Apocalypse of Peter, for example, tells how Peter saw people running toward him and his fellow apostles, threatening them with stones "as if they would kill us." Peter immediately appealed to the risen Jesus—probably in prayer—who told his terrified disciple to

"put your hands over your eyes, and tell what you see." But when I had done it, I did not see anything. I said, "No one sees [this way]." Again he told me, "Do it again." And there came into me fear and joy, for I saw a new light, greater than the light of day.[80]

During a moment suspended in time, while Peter hears the crowd shouting, he is shocked to see a vision of Jesus being crucified. After he cries out in fear and anguish, Peter learns from the "living Jesus" that what is spiritual cannot die. Finally, an astonished Peter sees a vision of Jesus "glad and laughing on the cross . . . and he was filled with a holy spirit . . . and there was a great, ineffable light around them, and a multitude of ineffable and invisible angels blessing them."[81] The anonymous author of the Apocalypse of Peter says that this vision encouraged Peter to face his own death with equanimity, knowing that the spirit within him may overcome death, as those facing persecution in later generations might do as well.

But how are visions received, and which are divinely inspired? Practically speaking, who is to judge? This central—and perplexing—question is what Christians since ancient times have called the problem of discerning spirits: how to tell which apparent inspirations come from God, which from the power of evil, and which from an overheated imagination. Although most people at the time—Jews, pagans, and Christians alike—assumed that the divine reveals itself in dreams, many people then, as now, recognized that dreams may also express only wishes and hopes, and that some may lead to fatal delusions. We have seen that Irenaeus recognized God's power in certain prophets, healers, and teachers, perhaps especially in those whose teaching agreed with what many Christians accepted in common. In others, however, he saw Satan at work—for example, in the case of Marcus, whom he called "Satan's apostle" and accused of inventing visions in order to deceive his followers and to exploit them for sexual favors and money.

In the Gospel of Mary Magdalene, discovered in Egypt in 1896, the apostles Andrew and Peter raise the same questions that troubled Irenaeus—but this time we hear a response from the visionary's point of view. The Gospel of Mary dramatizes how certain group leaders—here represented by the apostles Peter and Andrew—sometimes attacked and denounced those who claimed to see visions. Although the opening is lost, what we have of the Gospel of Mary begins with a vision in which the risen Jesus tells his disciples, "The Son of Man is *within you.* Follow after him! Those who seek him will find him. Go, then, and preach the gospel of the kingdom." Yet most of the disciples, apparently at a loss to find the divine within themselves, "were grieved, and wept greatly," terrified that they would be killed as Jesus was. Then Mary stood up, spoke, and "turned their hearts to the good":

> Do not weep, and do not grieve nor be afraid, for his grace will be with you completely, and will protect you. But rather let us praise his greatness, for he has prepared us, and has turned us into human beings.[82]

Then Peter says to Mary: "Sister, we know that the Savior loved you more than the rest of women. Tell us the words of the Savior which you remember—which you know but we do not, nor have we heard them."[83] Peter apparently expects to hear things that Jesus had said at times when he himself was absent. But Mary startles Peter by saying that she knows not only what Peter did not happen to hear but also what Jesus *chose* not to tell him: "What is hidden from you I will tell you." So, she continues, "I saw the Lord today in a vision," and she says that she was so astonished that she immediately asked him how visions occur:

> "How does one who sees the vision see it—through the soul, or through the spirit?" The Savior answered and said, "One does not see through the soul, nor through the spirit, but the mind which is between the two: that is what sees the vision."[84]

After hearing that visions come through the *mind*, or *consciousness*, Mary turns her attention to what the vision shows her. At this crucial point the papyrus text is broken, and much is lost; what remains is a fragment in which, as in the Dialogue of the Savior, Jesus reveals what happens after death. He explains that the soul encounters "seven powers of wrath," which challenge it, saying, "Whence do you come, killer of humans, and where are you going, conqueror of space?" Through this vision, Jesus teaches the soul how to respond, so that it may overcome these hostile powers.

When Mary stops speaking, an argument breaks out:

When Mary had said this, she fell silent, since it was to this point that the Savior had spoken with her. But Andrew answered and said to the brethren, "Say what you will about what she has said. I, at least, do not believe that the Savior said this, for certainly these teachings are strange ideas."[85]

Andrew's brother Peter adds: "Did he really speak with a woman without our knowledge, and not openly? Are we supposed to turn and listen to *her*? Did he love her more than *us*?"

Then Mary wept, and said to Peter, "My brother Peter, what do you think? Do you think that I made this up myself in my heart, or that I am lying about the Savior?" Levi answered and said to Peter, "Peter, you have always been hot tempered. Now I see you contending against the woman as our enemies do. But if the Savior made her worthy, who are you, indeed, to reject her? Surely the Savior knows her very well. That is why he loved her more than us. Rather, let us be ashamed, and . . . preach the gospel."[86]

Thus the author of the Gospel of Mary differs from Irenaeus about how to distinguish genuine visions. For when Irenaeus confronted a prophet he mistrusted, like Marcus, he might well have said what Peter and Andrew said to Mary, accusing those who claimed to have received visions of having "strange ideas" or of "making them up."

Irenaeus may have realized as he wrestled with this problem that it was nothing new; some of Israel's ancient prophets had asked—and been asked—the same questions. When Jeremiah, for example, predicted that war with Babylonia (c. 580 B.C.E.) would end in Israel's defeat, prophets who had predicted victory accused him of false prophecy. Jeremiah protested that he spoke only what came "from the mouth of the Lord" and accused his opponents of speaking lies that came "from their own mouths." So, he wrote,

> The Lord himself said to me, "I have heard what the prophets have said . . . who say, 'I have dreamed, I have dreamed.' See, I am against the prophets, says the Lord, who use *their own tongues*, and say, 'Says the Lord.' See, I am against the prophets, says the Lord, who *use their own tongues and prophesy lying dreams*, says the Lord, and who tell them, and who lead my people astray by their lies and wickedness, when I did not send them, nor did I command them or speak to them. They are prophesying to you *a lying vision, worthless divination, and the deceit of their own minds.*"[87]

Thus Jeremiah dismisses as worthless whatever comes from the prophets' "own mouths," "their own dreams," and "their own minds." Irenaeus, who has Marcus in mind, agrees, and adds what he learned from his anonymous Christian mentor, whom he calls "that divine elder and preacher of the truth"—false prophecy, especially Marcus's, comes from Satan.

Irenaeus adopted from Israel's prophetic tradition a second way of distinguishing which prophecies come from God: the conviction that the truth of oracles is revealed by events that bear them out. When Babylonian armies defeated Israel, Jeremiah's followers, convinced that this event proved his divine inspiration, collected his prophecies—having discarded those of his opponents—and added them to the sacred collection that would become the Hebrew Bible.

Followers of Jesus of Nazareth had made similar claims, as Irenaeus well knew. The author of the Gospel of Matthew, for example, insists that David, Isaiah, and Jeremiah had predicted specific events that happened at the time of Jesus, five hundred to a thousand years after the prophecies were written; thus these events demonstrate a divine plan. Many scholars today, however, suggest that the correspondence between prophecy and event that Matthew describes shows that he sometimes tailored his narrative to fit the prophecies. Matthew found, for example, the following oracle in the writings of the prophet Zechariah:

> Rejoice greatly . . . O daughter of Jerusalem! Behold, your king comes to you; triumphant and victorious is he; humble, and *riding on a donkey, [and] on a colt, the foal of a donkey.*[88]

Matthew read this passage as a prediction of how Jesus entered Jerusalem at Passover, but apparently he did not notice that Zechariah repeated the final phrases only for poetic effect. Consequently he wrote in his gospel that, when Jesus was preparing to enter Jerusalem, he ordered his disciples to bring him *both* a donkey and a colt. So, Matthew wrote, "the disciples went and did as Jesus had directed them; they brought *the donkey and the colt,* and put their clothes *on them,* and he sat *on them.*"[89] (The gospels of Mark and Luke, by contrast, agree that Jesus entered Jerusalem riding not on *two* animals but on a single colt.) Matthew did not intend to mislead his readers; what probably motivated him to correlate prophecy with event in this way was his conviction that, since Jesus *was* the messiah, his coming *must* have fulfilled the ancient prophecies.

Yet from the first century to the present, "arguments from prophecy" have persuaded many people; apparently including Irenaeus's mentor, The philosopher Justin Martyr, who wrote that, as a young student seeking truth (c. 140 c.e.), he had become disillusioned with one philosophy teacher after another—first a Stoic, then a Peripatetic, a Pythagorean teacher, and a disciple of Plato. Finally he concluded that the human mind by itself was incapable of finding truth and asked in dismay, "Should anyone, then, employ a teacher? For how could anyone be helped, if there is no truth even in them?" Justin writes that one day, as he was walking along the shore and thinking about these questions, he met an old man who told him about the Hebrew prophets, and how their ancient oracles had been proven true by events that had happened when Jesus came. The old man explained that

> there existed, long before now, certain men more ancient than all those who are regarded as philosophers—men both righteous and beloved by God who spoke by the divine spirit, and foretold events which would take place, and are now taking place. They are called prophets. These alone both saw and proclaimed the truth . . . being filled with the holy spirit. They did not use [logical] demonstration in their writings, since they were witnesses to truth

beyond such demonstration . . . and those events which
have happened and are happening now, compel you to
assent to what they say.[90]

"After he had said these things," Justin said, "he went away . . .
and I have not seen him since. But immediately a fire was kin-
dled in my soul, and a love of the prophets, and of those people
who are friends of Christ, possessed me."[91]

Justin met with a group of these people, and eventually received baptism in the name of the "holy spirit, who through the
prophets foretold everything about Jesus," and who, he later
wrote, illuminated his mind. Then, having become a "Christian
philosopher," he offered to prove to a Jewish philosopher named
Trypho that "we have not believed empty fables, or words without any foundation, but words filled with the spirit of God, and
great with power, and flourishing with grace."[92] Although he
says that Trypho's companions "laughed and shouted rudely"
when they heard this, Justin offered what he believed was in-
controvertible proof. He explained to Trypho, for example, that
the prophet Isaiah had foretold that "a virgin shall conceive and
bear a son"[93]—a miracle that Matthew says occurred nearly five
hundred years later, when Mary gave birth to Jesus. Justin adds
that other prophets, including David, Isaiah, and Zechariah, had
predicted in detail Jesus' birth, his final entry into Jerusalem,
the betrayal by Judas, and his crucifixion. Justin says that when
he engaged Trypho in public debate, he carefully set forth correlations between specific prophecies and the events that he
believed fulfilled them—correlations impossible to explain, he
argued, apart from divinely inspired prophecy, and God's intervention in human history.

But those who criticize such "proof from prophecy" suggest that Christians like Justin argue fallaciously—for example, by mistaking a misleading translation for a miracle. The author of the Gospel of Matthew, for example, apparently reading Isaiah's prophecy in Greek translation, took it to mean that "a *virgin* [*parthenos* in Greek] shall conceive." Justin himself acknowledges that Jewish interpreters, arguing with Jesus' followers, pointed out that what the prophet had actually written in the original Hebrew was simply that "a *young woman* [*almah*] shall conceive and bear a son"—apparently predicting immediate events expected in the royal succession.[94]

Yet Justin and Irenaeus, like many Christians to this day, remained unconvinced by such arguments, and believed instead that ancient prophecies predicted Jesus' birth, death, and resurrection, and that their divine inspiration has been proven by actual events. Unbelievers often find these proofs far-fetched, but for believers they demonstrate God's "history of salvation." Justin staked his life on this conviction, and believed that he had given up philosophical speculation for truth as empirically verifiable as that of the scientist whose experiments turn out as predicted.

Since Irenaeus saw the proof from prophecy as one way to resolve the problem of how to tell which prophecies—and which revelations—come from God, he added certain writings of "the apostles" to those of "the prophets," since he, like Justin, believed that together these constitute indispensable witnesses to truth. Like other Christians of their time, Justin and Irenaeus, when they spoke of "the Scriptures," had in mind primarily the Hebrew Bible: what we call the New Testament had not yet been assembled. Their conviction that God's truth is revealed in the

events of salvation history provides the essential link between
the Hebrew Bible and what Justin called "the apostles' mem-
oirs," which we know as the gospels of the New Testament.

It was Irenaeus, so far as we can tell, who became the prin-
cipal architect of what we call the four gospel canon, the framework that includes in the New Testament collection the gospels
of Matthew, Mark, Luke, and John. First Irenaeus denounces
various Christian groups that settle on only one gospel, like the
Ebionite Christians, who, he says, use only Matthew, or followers of Marcion, who use only Luke. Equally mistaken, Irenaeus
continues, are those who invoke many gospels. Certain Christians, he says, declared that certain Christians "boast that they
have more gospels than there really are . . . but really, they have
no gospel which is not full of blasphemy."[95] Irenaeus resolved to
hack down the forest of "apocryphal and illegitimate" writings—
writings like the Secret Book of James and the Gospel of Mary—
and leave only four "pillars" standing.[96] He boldly declared that
"the gospel," which contains all truth, can be supported by only
these four "pillars"—namely, the gospels attributed to Matthew,
Mark, Luke, and John. To defend his choice, he declared that "it
is not possible that there can be either more or fewer than four,"
for "just as there are four regions of the universe, and four prin-
cipal winds," the church itself requires "only four pillars."[97] Furthermore, just as the prophet Ezekiel envisioned God's throne
borne up by four living creatures, so the divine Word of God is
supported by this "four formed gospel." (Following his lead,
Christians in later generations took the faces of these four "living creatures"—the lion, the bull, the eagle, and the man—as
symbols of the four evangelists.) What makes these gospels
trustworthy, he claimed, is that their authors, who he believed

included Jesus' disciples Matthew and John, actually *witnessed* the events they related; similarly, he added, Mark and Luke, being followers of Peter and Paul, wrote down only what they had heard from the apostles themselves.

Few New Testament scholars today would agree with Irenaeus; we do not know who actually wrote these gospels, any more than we know who wrote the gospels of Thomas or Mary; all we know is that all of these "gospels" are attributed to disciples of Jesus. Nevertheless, as the next chapters will show, Irenaeus not only welded the Gospel of John to the far more widely quoted gospels of Matthew and Luke but praised John as the greatest gospel. For Irenaeus, John was not the *fourth* gospel, as Christians call it today, but the *first* and *foremost* of the gospels, because he believed that John alone understood who Jesus really is—God in human form. What God revealed in that extraordinary moment when he "became flesh" trumped any revelations received by mere human beings—even prophets and apostles, let alone the rest of us.

Irenaeus could not, of course, stop people from seeking revelation of divine truth—nor, as we have seen, did he intend to do so. After all, religious traditions survive through time only as their adherents relive and reimagine them and, in the process, continually transform them. But, from his own time to the present, Irenaeus and his successors among church leaders did strive to compel all believers to subject themselves to the "fourfold gospel" and to what he called apostolic tradition. Henceforth all "revelations" endorsed by Christian leaders would have to agree with the gospels set forth in what would become the New Testament. Throughout the centuries, of course, these gospels have given rise to an extraordinary range of Christian art, music, poetry, theology, and legend. But even the church's most gifted saints, like Teresa of Avila and John of the Cross, would be careful not to transgress—much less transcend—these boundaries. To this day, many traditionally minded Christians continue to believe that whatever trespasses canonical guidelines must be "lies and wickedness" that come either from the evil of the human heart or from the devil.

Yet Irenaeus recognized that even banishing all "secret writings" and creating a canon of four gospel accounts could not, by itself, safeguard the Christian movement. What if some who read the "right" gospels read them in the wrong way—or in *many* wrong ways? What if Christians interpreted these same gospels to inspire—or, as the bishop might say, to spawn—new "heresies"? This is what happened in Irenaeus's congregation—and, as we shall see, he responded by working to construct what he called orthodox (literally, "straight-thinking") Christianity.

†ōtōtōt†

THE CANON OF TRUTH
AND THE TRIUMPH
OF JOHN

People engaged in spiritual exploration often are especially attracted to the Gospel of John; for, although written with great simplicity—and, apparently, to advocate faith—this gospel shines with paradox, mystery, and hints of deeper meaning. Thus T. S. Eliot, moved by its opening lines, wrote these in response:

> And the light shone in darkness and
> Against the Word the unstilled world still whirled
> About the center of the silent Word.[1]

Some four centuries before Eliot, another poet, the son of converted Jews, an intense young Spanish monk who would become a saint and mystic, chose John's name as his own, calling himself John of the Cross. Now, largely because of the Nag Hammadi discoveries, we can see that, nearly two thousand years ago, many of John's earliest readers also responded to this gospel in surprising and imaginative ways.

How did those Christians whom Irenaeus calls "evil interpreters" read John and the other Scriptures—and why did he oppose what they found there? Irenaeus warns that these people "have cast truth aside";[2] they introduce lies that entice and delude naïve believers, but to many people their obvious fictions actually seem true. Irenaeus says that the Christian poet and teacher Valentinus, his disciple Ptolemy, and others like them have invented all kinds of myths about what happened "in the beginning," and even *before* the beginning of the world, and how the unknown Source of all being, which these Christians sometimes call the primal Father and other times call Silence—since there are no words to describe this Source—first poured forth streams of divine energies, both masculine and feminine, whose dynamic interaction brought forth the universe. Some followers of Ptolemy go on to say that divine Wisdom came forth "in the beginning" and participated with God to bring forth the universe, as described in Genesis 1 through 3.

Irenaeus may not have known that such questions were widely discussed in certain Jewish circles among teachers and their disciples, who apparently influenced the questions that teachers like Valentinus and Ptolemy asked, as well as their interpretation of passages from Israel's Scriptures—especially Genesis, the Psalms, and the oracles of Isaiah and Proverbs.

We know little of Valentinus himself, since only a few fragments of his writing survive,[3] but he, too, wrote a poem reflecting on the mystery of how the visible universe emerges from the invisible Source, as Genesis 1:2 says, after "the spirit moved above the depth":

> All things I see suspended through spirit;
> All things borne along through spirit;
> Flesh depending on soul,
> Soul bound to air,
> Air depending on ether,
> From the depth, fruit brought forth,
> From the mother's womb, a child.[4]

At the same time, Valentinus and his disciples were among the first, perhaps a hundred years before the New Testament canon was established, to place these newer "apostolic" writings along with Genesis and the prophets, and to revere the authority of Jesus' sayings as equal to or even above that of Israel's Scriptures.[5] Ptolemy even wrote in a letter to Flora, an aristocratic Roman woman who studied with him, that Jesus' sayings offer "the *only* unerring way to comprehend reality."[6] In discussing divine mysteries, Irenaeus says that Ptolemy and members of his circle often cited passages from Paul's letters and the "sayings of the Lord" known to us from Matthew and Luke; but what they quoted repeatedly, "making the fullest possible use"[7] of it, was the Gospel of John—which was, in fact, their favorite. When Irenaeus decided to arm himself against these teachers by reading their commentaries and confronting their authors, he may have known that Heracleon, whom he calls Valentinus's "most respected" disciple, had written a famous *Commentary on John*—which is, so far as we know, the earliest commentary written on *any* New Testament book.[8]

When I first heard about Heracleon's commentary, I wondered: Why would anyone bother to write a *commentary* on a gospel written so clearly? And what would attract a *heretic* to a gospel that was to become the touchstone of orthodoxy? Later, after studying the newly discovered sources, I saw that, by putting my questions this way, I had unconsciously adopted Irenaeus's terminology and incorporated his viewpoint. For what he did, with remarkable success, was convince Christians that his reading of John's gospel—or any gospel, for that matter—was the only correct reading, and that his approach was the "canonical" scriptural interpretation. Irenaeus, as we shall see, insisted on what he called the "canon of truth" and rejected the kind of exegesis which he said was "current among Greek philosophers,"[9] such as certain Stoics who read Homer's poems allegorically, taking gods like Zeus and Hera to represent elements of the natural universe, and such as followers of Plato, who claimed to find in Homer's poems allusions to teachings such as the transmigration of the soul.[10] Irenaeus, alarmed by what Valentinus's disciples were doing, warns believers to beware of approaching their own sacred texts in such ways. On the contrary, he declares that, wherever possible, one must discern the obvious meaning; and whenever a certain passage seems ambiguous or difficult, one's understanding should be guided by those passages whose meaning seems clear.[11]

Heretics, Irenaeus warns, read wildly, concentrating on the enigmas, mysteries, and parables they find in the Scriptures, rather than on passages that seem plain; often they read incoherently, or in conflict with the obvious meaning of the text.[12] Although some write commentaries, many more respond to what they find in Genesis, in Isaiah's oracles, Paul's letters, the

Psalms, and the gospels by coming up with songs, poems, visions, and "revelations" of their own—even liturgical dance. As we shall see, the texts discovered at Nag Hammadi bear out Irenaeus's suspicions, as well as his conviction about what was at stake: what is spiritual truth, and how it may be discerned.

Let us look, then, at a few of these "wild readings" to see how the Gospel of John became a center of controversy. Despite its simplicity of style, few readers have found John's gospel easy to understand. Especially in the context of the synoptic gospels, even its earliest admirers noticed, for example, that it sometimes contradicts Matthew, Mark, and Luke. For example, as we noted, John begins with the story of Jesus attacking the money changers and merchants in the Temple, a scene whose violence John increases by adding that Jesus "knotted a whip out of small cords" and wielded it as he "drove them all out of the Temple, and the sheep and the oxen, and poured out the changers' money, and overthrew the tables."[13] The other gospels, as we have seen, all place this incident at the end of Jesus' life, when it must logically have happened, since this act, according to Matthew, Mark, and Luke, was what impelled the chief priests to have Jesus arrested and turned over to the Roman authorities to be killed. When Origen, the brilliant Egyptian "father of the church" (later accused of heresy himself), was asked about this, he explained, as we have seen, that although "John does not always tell the truth *literally*, he always tells the truth *spiritually*"[14]—that is, symbolically. Origen even suggests that the holy spirit inserted such contradictions into John's gospel in order to startle the reader into asking what they mean, and to show that these stories are not meant to be taken literally; he agreed with Valentinus and his disciples that the reader has to plunge beyond the shimmering surface of John's words—or those of any of "the scriptures"—to seek their hidden meanings.

Valentinus, a poet himself, loved the power of biblical images, especially John's. Though orthodox Christians later sought to destroy his teachings, the surviving fragments show that he took the story of the cleansing of the Temple, for example, as a parable showing how, when God shines into our hearts, he shatters and transforms what he finds there to make us fit dwellings for the holy spirit.[15] Another fragment suggests that Valentinus's own spiritual awakening occurred when he received a revelatory dream in which a newborn child appeared and said to him, "I am the *logos*"[16]—in John's language, the divine *word* revealed in human form.

Let us look at several examples of what Irenaeus calls "evil exegesis," and then consider what he finds objectionable. Irenaeus identifies Valentinus as the author of what he calls the Gospel of Truth, and if this is the same one discovered at Nag Hammadi, we now can see, for the first time, how Valentinus praised the "hidden mystery, Jesus the Christ."[17] Whether written by Valentinus or, more likely, by one of his followers, the Gospel of Truth depicts a world devoid of God as a nightmare, a world like the one Matthew Arnold described nearly two thousand years later:

. . . the world, which seems
to lie before us like a land of dreams,
so various, so beautiful, so new,
hath really neither joy, nor love, nor light, nor certitude, nor
    peace, nor help for pain;
and we are here as on a darkling plain

swept with confused alarms of struggle and flight
where ignorant armies clash by night.[18]

The Gospel of Truth, too, pictures human existence, apart from
God, as a nightmare, in which people feel

> as if . . . they were fleeing, or, without strength they come
> from having chased after others; or they are . . . striking
> blows, or . . . receiving blows themselves; or they have
> fallen from high places, or they take off into the air,
> though they do not even have wings; . . . or as if people
> were murdering them, though there is no one pursuing
> them, or they themselves are killing their neighbors, for
> they have been stained with their blood.[19]

But *unlike* Arnold, the author of this gospel believes that we
can awaken from horror to discover God's presence here and
now; and when we wake up, the terror recedes, for the divine
breath—the spirit—runs after us, "and, having extended a hand,
lift[s] [us] up to stand on [our] feet."[20] Thus, the Gospel of Truth
continues, echoing John's prologue, the *"word* of the Father, . . .
Jesus of the infinite sweetness . . . goes forth into all things, sup-
porting all things," and finally restores all things to God, "bring-
ing them back into the Father, and into the Mother."[21]

The Gospel of Truth also says that what we see in Jesus—or
God—depends on what we need to see, and what we are capable of seeing. For although the divine is "ineffable, unimaginable," our understanding is bound by words and images, which
can either limit or extend what we perceive. So, although God

is, of course, neither masculine nor feminine, when invoking the image of God the Father, this author also speaks of God the Mother. Moreover, while drawing upon images of Jesus familiar from the gospels of Matthew and Luke (the "good shepherd")[22] and from Paul, who speaks of wisdom's "hidden mystery,"[23] as well as from John ("the word of the Father"), this author offers other visions of Jesus as well. Acknowledging that believers commonly see Jesus "nailed to the cross" as an image recalling sacrificial death, this author suggests seeing him instead as "fruit on a tree"—none other than the "tree of knowledge" in Paradise.[24] But instead of destroying those who eat the fruit, as Adam was destroyed, *this* fruit, "Jesus the Christ," conveys *genuine* knowledge—not intellectual knowledge but the knowing of mutual recognition (a word related to the Greek term *gnosis*)—to those whom God "discovers . . . in himself, and they discover him in themselves."[25]

This gospel takes its name from the opening line: "The gospel of truth is joy, to those who receive from the Father the grace of knowing him,"[26] for it transforms our understanding of God and ourselves. Those who receive this gospel no longer "think of [God] as petty, nor harsh, nor wrathful"—not, that is, as some biblical stories portray him—"but as a being without evil," loving, full of tranquillity, gracious, and all-knowing.[27] The Gospel of Truth pictures the holy spirit as God's breath, and envisions the Father first breathing forth the entire universe of living beings ("his children are his fragrant breath"), then drawing all beings back into the embrace of their divine source.[28] Meanwhile, he urges those who "discover God in themselves, and themselves in God" to transform *gnosis* into action:

> Speak the truth to those who seek it,
> And speak of understanding to those who have
>   committed sin through error;
> Strengthen the feet of those who have stumbled;
> Extend your hands to those who are sick;
> Feed those who are hungry;
> Give rest to those who are weary;
> And raise up those who wish to rise.[29]

Those who care for others and do good "do the will of the Father."

A second example of what Irenaeus calls "evil interpretation"—the so-called Round Dance of the Cross—illustrates what he means by "heretics" who often add "their own inventions" to the gospels. The anonymous follower of Valentinus who wrote the Round Dance offers to fill in a scene missing from John's gospel, in which Jesus chanted and danced with his disciples "on the night he was betrayed."[30] The Round Dance author notes that John's gospel *leaves out* an account of the last supper in which Jesus tells his disciples to eat bread as his body and drink wine as his blood—that scene which Matthew, Luke, and Paul all regard as central, for it shows believers how to celebrate the "Lord's supper." But in John's account of that night, something quite different happened. After dinner, according to John, Jesus

> got up from the table, took off his outer robe, and tied a cloth around himself. Then he poured water into a basin and began to wash the disciples' feet and to wipe them with the cloth that was tied around him.[31]

John means to say that this act is significant—even necessary—for anyone who wants to share communion with Jesus, for as he recounts it, when Peter protested that his teacher must not wash his feet like a slave, Jesus told him that "you do not now recognize what I am doing, but later you will understand," and added, "Unless I wash you, you have no share in me."[32] From ancient times to the present, many Christians have reenacted *this* scene as if it, like the last supper, offered directions for a ritual; so, on the Thursday before Easter, the pope of the Roman Catholic Church takes the role of Jesus and ritually washes the feet of his cardinals. Within the Church of Jesus Christ of Latter-day Saints, the church's president washes the feet of the Mormon "elders"; and to this day many other Christian groups—various Orthodox churches and many Protestant groups, including some Baptists and Pentecostalists—do likewise.

Whoever wrote the Round Dance of the Cross boldly revised John's account of that night by adding a different episode—apparently meant to be kept secret. In the Round Dance, which is found in the Acts of John, a second-century collection of stories and traditions inspired by John's gospel, John begins the story of Jesus' final night where the gospel account leaves off, and says that Jesus invited his disciples to dance and sing with him:

> Before he was arrested . . . he assembled us all, and said, "Before I am delivered to them, let us sing a hymn to the Father, and so go to meet what lies before us." So he told us to form a circle, holding one another's hands, and he himself stood in the middle and said, "Answer Amen to me."[33]

Then, as the disciples circled him, dancing, Jesus began to chant
a hymn in words that echo the Gospel of John:

> "Glory to you, Father." And we, circling around him,
>   answered him, "Amen."
> "Glory to you, Logos; glory to you, Grace." "Amen."
> "Glory to you, Spirit; glory to you, Holy One. . . ." "Amen."
> "We praise you, Father; we thank you, Light, in whom
>   dwells no darkness." "Amen. . . ."
> "I am a light to you who see me." "Amen."
> "I am a mirror to you who know me." "Amen."
> "I am a door to you who knock upon me." "Amen."
> "I am a way to you, the traveler." "Amen."[34]

Although the phrase about the mirror could have come straight
from the Gospel of Thomas, the primary source for the last two,
as well as many of the others, is the Gospel of John.

Whoever composed this hymn, then, clearly found in John's
gospel inspiration for the kind of teaching we more often associate with Thomas; for here Jesus invites his disciples to see
themselves in him:

> "[W]hich I am about to suffer is your own. For you could by no
> means have understood what you suffer, unless I had
> been sent to you as word [logos] by the Father . . . if you
> knew how to suffer, you would be able not to suffer."[35]

Thus, in the Round Dance of the Cross, Jesus says that he suffers
in order to reveal the nature of human suffering, and to teach

the paradox that the Buddha also taught: that those who become aware of suffering simultaneously find release from it. Yet
he also tells them to join in the cosmic dance: " 'Whoever dances
belongs to the whole.' 'Amen.' 'Whoever does not dance does
not know what happens.' 'Amen.' "[36]

Those who loved the Acts of John apparently celebrated the
eucharist by chanting these words, holding hands, and circling
in this dance to celebrate together the mystery of Jesus' suffering, and their own—and some Christians celebrate it thus to
this day. In the Acts of John, John tells his fellow disciples that it
is not "strange or paradoxical" that each of them sees Jesus in
different ways, for he explains that what anyone can see depends on that person's expectations and capacity. Once, he says,
Peter and Andrew asked John and James about the young child
they saw calling them from the shore,

> and my brother said . . . to me, "John, what does he want,
> this child on the shore who called us?" And I said, "Which
> child?" And he answered me, "The one beckoning to us."
> And I said, "Because of the long watch at sea, you are not
> seeing well, brother James. Don't you see the man stand-
> ing there who is handsome, with a joyful face?" But he
> said to me, "I do not see him, my brother; but let us dis-
> embark, and see what this means."[37]

John adds, "at another time, he took me and James and Peter
onto a mountain where he used to pray, and we saw him illuminated by a light that no human language could describe." Later,
"Again he took the three of us onto a mountain, and we saw him

praying at a distance." John says, however, that "since he loved me, I went up quietly to him, as if he did not see, and I stood there looking at his back." Suddenly, John says, he saw Jesus as Moses once saw the Lord—"he was wearing no clothes . . . and did not look like a human being at all . . . his feet shone with light so brilliant that it lit up the earth, and his head reached into heaven, so terrifying that I cried out"—whereupon Jesus immediately turned, was transformed back into the man that John could easily recognize, and rebuked John in words Jesus speaks to Thomas in John's own gospel: "John, do not be faithless, but believe."[38]

The Gospel of John inspired yet another example of "evil exegesis"—the famous and influential Secret Book of John, which Irenaeus apparently read, and which another anonymous Christian wrote, in John's name, apparently as a sequel to the gospel. The Secret Book opens after Jesus' death, when "John, the brother of James, the son of Zebedee," walking toward the Temple, is accosted by a Pharisee, who charges that "this Nazarene" has deceived John and his fellow believers, "filled your ears with lies, closed your hearts, and turned you from the traditions of your fathers."[39] John turns away from the Temple and flees to a desolate place in the mountains, "grieving greatly in [his] heart." There, as he struggles alone with fear and doubt, he says that "suddenly the heavens opened, and the whole creation shone, and the world was shaken."[40] John is astonished and terrified to see an unearthly light, in which changing forms appear, and to hear Jesus' voice saying, "John, John, why are you astonished, and why are you afraid? . . . I am the one who is with you always. I am the Father; I am the Mother; and I am the Son."[41] After a moment of shock, John recognizes Jesus as the one who radiates the light of God and appears in various forms, including Father, Son, and Holy Spirit—the last envisioned as feminine (suggested by the gender of the Hebrew term for spirit, *ruah*) and so as divine Mother.

But after Jesus consoles John with this vision, he says that "the God and Father of all things" cannot actually be apprehended in anthropomorphic images, since God is "the invisible one who is above all things, who exists as incorruption, in the pure light into which no eye may look,"[42] invisible, unimaginable, wholly beyond human comprehension. How, then, can one speak of God at all? To answer this question, the author of the Secret Book borrows the language of John's gospel: "To the point that I am able to comprehend him—for who will ever be able to comprehend him? . . . [God] is the light, the one who gives the light; the life, the one who gives the life."[43] Yet what follows, as we shall see in the next chapter, is a remarkable dialogue in which John questions the risen Savior, who gives him a breathtaking and wildly imaginative account of what happened "in the beginning"—mysteries hidden before creation within the divine being, the origin of evil, and the nature and spiritual destiny of humankind.

Of all the instances Irenaeus offers of "evil exegesis," however, his prime example is part of a commentary on John that asks questions similar to those asked in the Secret Book—what John's gospel reveals about "the origin of all things." The author of this commentary, traditionally identified as Ptolemy,[44] says that "John, the disciple of the Lord, wanting to set forth the origin of all things, how the Father brought forth all things,"[45] reveals in his opening lines—although in a way hidden from the casual reader—the original structure of divine being. This, he says, is

the "primary ogdoad," which consists of the first eight emana-
tions of divine energy, rather similar to what kabbalists later
will call the divine *sephirot;* thus, when Valentinus and his disciples read the opening of John's gospel, they envisioned God,
the divine *word,* and Jesus Christ as, so to speak, waves of divine
energy flowing down from above, from the great waterfall to
the local creek.

Irenaeus rejects this attempt to find hidden meaning in
John's prologue and explains to his reader that he has quoted
this commentary at length so that "you may see, beloved, the
method by which those using it deceive themselves, and abuse
the Scriptures by trying to support their own invention from
them."[46] Had John meant to set forth the primordial structure of
divine being, Irenaeus says, he would have made his meaning
clear; thus "the fallacy of their interpretation is obvious";[47] and
he then, as we shall see, offers the *true* interpretation of John's
gospel.

Yet Irenaeus undertook his massive, five-volume *Refutation
and Overthrow of Falsely So-Called Knowledge* precisely because he
knew that many people might find his conclusions far from obvious. Worse, they might well see him and his opponents as
rival theologians squabbling about interpretation, rather than
as orthodox Christians against heretics. While his opponents
say he reads only the surface, he replies that all of them say different things; not one of them agrees with another, not even
with their own teachers; on the contrary, "each one of them
comes up with something new every day,"[48] as do writers and
artists today, for whom originality is evidence of genuine insight. For Irenaeus, however, innovation proved that one had
abandoned the true gospel. The problem he faced, then, was

how to sort out all those lies, fictions, and fantasies. How to distinguish true from false?

Irenaeus says that there is only one way to be safe from error: go back to what you first learned, and "hold *unmoving* in [your] heart the canon of truth received in baptism."[49] He assumes that his audience knows what this canon is: "This faith, which the church, even when scattered throughout the whole world . . . received from the apostles," and which, he specifies, includes faith in

> one God, Father almighty, creator of heaven and earth, and the seas . . . and in one Christ Jesus, the son of God, who became incarnate for our salvation, and in the holy spirit . . . and the birth from a virgin, and the suffering, and the resurrection from the dead, and the heavenly ascension in flesh . . . of our beloved Jesus Christ.[50]

True believers everywhere, he says, share this same faith.

Irenaeus's vision of a united and unanimous "catholic church" speaks more of what he hoped to create than what he actually saw in the churches he knew in Gaul, and those he had visited or heard about in his travels though Gaul, Asia Minor, and Italy. In those travels he encountered resistance from those he called heretics, and when he urged them to return to the simple baptismal faith, he says that they answered in words like this:

> We too, have accepted the faith you describe, and we have confessed the same things—faith in one God, in Jesus Christ, in the virgin birth and the resurrection—when we were baptized. But since that time, following Jesus' injunc-

tion to "seek, and you shall find," we have been striving to
go beyond the church's elementary precepts, hoping to at-
tain spiritual maturity.

Now that the discoveries at Nag Hammadi allow the
heretics—virtually for the first time—to speak for themselves,
let us look at the Gospel of Philip, to see how its author, a
Valentinian teacher, compares his own circle with that of those
he considers "simpler" Christian believers. This author, whom
we call Philip, and his circle apparently had received baptism in
a procedure similar to the one that the church father Justin
Martyr describes as customary in Rome;[51] that is, the initiate,
having repented of past sins, receives and affirms the teachings
of Jesus as taught by his followers, confesses the faith, and
promises to live accordingly. Then, led naked into the water, the
initiate is baptized as the divine names—God the Father; Jesus
Christ, his son; and the holy spirit—are pronounced; and finally,
dressed in fresh garments, the new Christian is anointed with
oil and invited to participate in the eucharist. Like Justin, Philip
says that baptism effects spiritual rebirth; "through this mystery
we are *born again* though the holy spirit."[52]

But unlike Justin—or any other early Christian writer known
to me—Philip then asks, *What happens—or doesn't happen*—when a
person undergoes baptism? Is baptism the same for everyone?
Philip suggests it is not. There are many people, he says, whose
baptism simply marks initiation; such a person "goes down into
the water and comes up without having received anything and
says 'I am a Christian.' "[53] But sometimes, Philip continues, the
person who undergoes baptism "receives the holy spirit . . . this
is what happens when one experiences a mystery."[54] What

makes the difference involves not only the mysterious gift of divine grace but also the initiate's capacity for spiritual understanding.

So, Philip writes, echoing Paul's Letter to the Galatians, many believers see themselves more as God's slaves than as God's children; but those who are baptized, like newborn infants, are meant to grow in faith toward hope, love, and understanding (*gnosis*):

> Faith is our earth, in which we take root; hope is the water through which we are nourished; love is the air through which we grow; *gnosis* is the light through which we become fully grown.[55]

Thus, he explains, those who first confess faith in the virgin birth later may come to a different understanding of what this means. Many believers, indeed, continue to take the virgin birth literally, as if Mary conceived apart from Joseph; "some say that Mary conceived through the holy spirit," but, Philip says, "they are in error."[56] For, he explains, "virgin birth" is not simply something that happened once to Jesus; rather, it refers to what may happen to everyone who is baptized and so "born again" through the "virgin who came down," that is, through the holy spirit.[57] Thus, as Jesus was born to Joseph and Mary, his human parents, and later was born *spiritually* when the holy spirit descended upon him at his baptism, so we, too, first born physically, may be "born again through the holy spirit" in baptism, so that "when we became Christians we came to have both a father and mother,"[58] that is, both the heavenly Father and the holy spirit.

But Philip says that many people, whom he calls "the apostles and the apostolic ones,"[59] are "in error," since they remain
oblivious of—even offended by—this mystery. Such people, he
continues, are also wrong about resurrection, since they take
this, too, as if it could be only a unique event in which Christ
died and rose bodily from the grave. Philip suggests instead
that Jesus' resurrection, like his virgin birth, is not only something that occurred in the past but is a paradigm of what happens to each person who undergoes spiritual transformation.
Philip quotes Paul's famous teaching on resurrection ("flesh and
blood shall not inherit the kingdom of God," I Corinthians 15:50)
to show that those who receive the holy spirit in baptism are
not only "born again" but also "raised from the dead."[60]

Someone might object, however, that this cannot be what resurrection means: didn't Jesus rise *in the flesh*? Philip answers that,
of course, "one must rise 'in this flesh,' since in this world everything exists in [the flesh]." But he challenges those who take bodily
resurrection literally. After all, he asks, "what is flesh?" In answer,
he quotes from John's gospel to show that when Jesus told his
disciples to "eat my flesh and drink my blood" (John 6:53), he
was speaking in metaphor, since what he meant was that they
were to partake of the sacred meal of bread and wine, which
conveys Jesus' "flesh," that is, Philip suggests, his divine *word*,
and his "blood," the holy spirit.[61]

Philip thus discriminates between nominal Christians—those
who claim to be Christians simply because they were baptized—
and those who, after baptism, are spiritually transformed. He
sees himself among the latter but does not congratulate himself
for belonging to a spiritual elite; instead, he concludes by anticipating that ultimately *all* believers will be transformed, if not

in this world then in eternity. Whoever undergoes such trans-formation, he says "no longer is a Christian, but a Christ."[62]

If Irenaeus read the Gospel of Philip, he must have sharply rejected such teaching; for, as we have seen, when he demands that the believer "hold *unmoving* in his heart the rule of truth received in baptism," he specifically includes the "birth from a virgin, the passion, and the resurrection from the dead . . . in the flesh of our beloved Jesus Christ, our Lord";[63] and, like many orthodox believers ever since, Irenaeus accepted these as unique, revelatory events through which Christ ensured human salvation. Were members of Philip's circle to answer that they confessed the same faith, Irenaeus would have replied, as he did to other Valentinian Christians, that although they "say the same things, they mean something different by them." Followers of Valentinus might readily have admitted that this was true; but, they asked him, what is *wrong* with that? "When we confess the same things as you, why do you call us heretics?"[64] No doubt their interpretations *differed* from his, and from each other's; but why did Irenaeus think that these differences actually *endangered* the church?

These questions are hard to answer, for although Irenaeus liked clear boundaries, he was not simply narrow-minded, and he was by no means intolerant of all difference. In fact, as he sought to realize his teacher Polycarp's vision of a *universal* church, he included as "apostolic" a wide range of traditions that spanned a century and a half and, he claimed, were shared by Christians scattered from Germany to Spain, Gaul to Asia Minor, and from Italy to Africa, Egypt, and Palestine. Irenaeus surely knew that the traditions he accepted—to say nothing of many more that he disagreed with but allowed—included the diversity of beliefs and practices that one would expect of what he called "the catholic church ... scattered throughout the whole world."[65]

In fact, Irenaeus encouraged his fellow believers to tolerate certain variations of viewpoint and practice. For example, he argued against those who accepted only *one* gospel, such as those he calls the Ebionites, who, he says, accepted only Matthew, and followers of Marcion, who accepted only Luke. And while his contemporary Tatian, who, like himself, was a student of Justin, attempted to harmonize the various gospels by rewriting them into one single, composite account, Irenaeus was the first, so far as we know, to urge believers to accept all *four* distinct gospels, despite their obvious differences, and to join them into the collage that he called the "four formed gospel." Furthermore, when Victor, bishop of Rome, demanded that all Christians in the capital city celebrate Easter on the same day, Irenaeus traveled to Rome to urge the bishop not to cause trouble for Greek-speaking Christians, who like Irenaeus himself, had emigrated from Asia Minor and traditionally celebrated Easter on a different day (as Greek, Russian, Ethiopic, Serbian, and Coptic Orthodox Christians still do).[66]

Given, then, that Irenaeus acknowledged a wide range of views and practices, at what point did he find "heterodoxy"—which literally means "different opinions"—*problematic*, and for what reasons? Why does he declare that the Gospel of Truth, like all the "heretical" gospels, "has nothing to do with the apostolic gospel" but is "full of blasphemy"?[67] Why does he insist that the Secret Book of John simply shows "the kind of lies the heretics invent"?[68] To answer these questions, we should recall that Irenaeus was not a theoretically minded philosopher engaging in theological debate so much as a young man thrust into leadership of the survivors of a group of Christians in Gaul after a violent and bloody persecution. As we have seen, Irenaeus could not forget that in Smyrna, where he had grown up in the household of Bishop Polycarp, his aged and renowned spiritual father had been hounded by the police, and after escaping and hiding in a country house, had been captured and brought back to the public amphitheater, where, as the mob shouted insults, he was stripped naked and burned alive. Then, as we noted, about twenty years later (c. 177), in Gaul, where Polycarp may have sent him to work as a missionary, Irenaeus had seen more violence against Christians, some of whom were lynched while dozens of others were arrested and tortured, many strangled to death in prison. According to *The Letters of the Churches of Lyons and Vienne*, some thirty to fifty who survived and refused to renounce their witness were torn apart by wild animals and killed by gladiators in a public spectacle attended by his fellow townspeople. And we have seen that only after the aged bishop Pothinus had died of torture and exposure in prison, Irenaeus, perhaps in his thirties, having somehow escaped arrest, apparently stepped in to serve as leader of those who were left.

As he did so, determined to consolidate these scattered believers and provide them the shelter of a community by joining them into the worldwide network Polycarp had envisioned as a "catholic" church, what concerned Irenaeus was whatever proved seriously divisive. What, then, *did* prove divisive? Irenaeus would have answered *heresy*—and because of the way he characterized it, historians traditionally have identified *orthodoxy* (which literally means "straight thinking") with a certain set of ideas and opinions, and heterodoxy (that is, "thinking other-wise") as an opposite set of ideas. Yet I now realize that we greatly oversimplify when we accept the traditional identifica-tion of *orthodoxy* and *heresy* solely in terms of the philosophical and theological content of certain ideas. What especially con-cerned Irenaeus was the way the activities of these "spiritual teachers" threatened Christian solidarity by offering *second bap-tism* to initiate believers into distinct groups *within* congrega-tions.

The author of the Gospel of Philip, as we have seen, *implicitly* divided the church by discriminating between those who, he says, are "in error" and those who have "come to know the truth"; but Irenaeus knew that many other followers of Valenti-nus divided the church *explicitly*. What he found most objection-able was not so much what they *said* as what they *did*—above all, that many offered believers a *second* baptism in a ritual they called *apolutrosis*—which could take many forms.[69] Irenaeus de-scribes precisely how they operated. First, they called them-selves "spiritual Christians" and attracted unwary people from what they called the "common" and "ecclesiastical" majority, inviting them into private meetings of their own. There they challenged the newcomers—and themselves—to question what their faith meant, and in the process they often discussed pas-sages from the Scriptures. Irenaeus may be speaking from his own experience when he complains that when someone objects to what they say or asks them to explain what they mean, "they claim that he is not a person capable of receiving the truth, since he has not received from above the capacity to under-stand"; thus, he says, "they really give him no answer." But when they find people who prove receptive, they engage them in a long period of preparation and finally declare that these are ready to receive *apolutrosis*, which enables them to move beyond the "common" community to join the more select circles of the spiritually mature. So, Irenaeus complains,

> they call those who belong to the church "common," and "ecclesiastic". . . and *if anyone gives himself up to them like a little sheep, and follows out their practice and their apolutrosis*, such a person is so elated that he imagines he . . . has already entered within the "fullness of God". . . and goes strutting around with a superior expression on his face, with all the pomposity of a cock.[70]

What Irenaeus found most distressing was that those who flocked to the groups gathered around teachers like Ptolemy often heard in these meetings that the baptism all Christians receive in common is, in fact, only the *first step* in the life of faith. Such teachers explained to newcomers that just as John the Baptist baptized with water those who repented, when they themselves first confessed faith in God and in Jesus, they too received, in effect, the "baptism of John" to cleanse them from sin. But such teachers also pointed out how, according to the gospel accounts of Mark, Matthew, and Luke, John the Baptist prophesied that Jesus himself would baptize his followers "with the holy spirit and with fire."[71] They pointed out, too, Jesus' saying that he had "another baptism with which to be baptized,"[72] and they explained that this means that those who advance on the spiritual path are to receive that *second* baptism.

Furthermore, they said, this higher baptism marks a major transition in the initiate's relationship with God. In their first baptism, believers have pledged to serve as Lord the God whom they revere as creator, and fear as divine lawgiver and judge; but now, Ptolemy and his disciples explained, having progressed beyond that level of understanding, they are to come to see God as Father, as Mother, Source of all being—in other words, as One who transcends all such images. Thus Ptolemy invites those who previously saw themselves as God's *servants*—or, more bluntly, his slaves—to come to understand themselves as God's *children*. To signal their release from slavery to become, in Paul's words, God's own children and heirs,[73] Ptolemy calls the second baptism *apolutrosis*, which means "redemption" or "release," alluding to the judicial process through which a slave became legally free.

When we look back to our examples of "evil interpretation," we can see that Irenaeus's characterization, however hostile, nevertheless is accurate. Those who wrote and treasured innovative works such as the Gospel of Truth, the Round Dance of the Cross, the Secret Book of John, and the Gospel of Philip were implicitly criticizing, intentionally or not, the faith of most believers. So, as we noted, Valentinus contrasts those who picture God as a "petty, jealous, and angry" with those who receive "the grace of knowing him" as a loving and compassionate Father. Many scholars believe that the Gospel of Truth was written as an inspirational talk to be delivered at some such baptism among Valentinus's followers, as those who come to know themselves as God's children also come to recognize one another, this gospel says, as "true brothers, upon whom the Father's love is poured out, and among whom He is fully present."[74] So, too, those who participated in the Round Dance of the Cross, circling in the dance and chanting "Amen!" in response to the person chanting Jesus' part, were celebrating their new relationship with Jesus, who here, as we noted, invites them to

see yourself in Me who am speaking, and, when you have seen what I do, keep silent about my mysteries. You who dance, consider what I do; for this human passion which I am about to suffer is your own.[75]

The dance celebration described in the Round Dance itself may have served as a form of *apolutrosis;* for while virtually all Christians first initiated newcomers through some kind of water baptism, Irenaeus says that these spiritual teachers had not come up with any single way of performing the second baptism: "It has no set form, and every teacher transmits it in his own way, as each is inclined; so there are as many kinds of *apolutrosis* as there are teachers of these mystical insights."[76]

Having carefully investigated these matters, he reports that some of them baptized initiates with water a second time, using different invocations:

Some . . . bring the initiates to water, and baptizing them, they say these words: *"in the name of the unknown Father of all being; into Truth, the mother of all things; into the One who descended on Jesus [the spirit];* into union; redemption [*apolutrosis*]; and communion with the powers."[77]

Others performed *apolutrosis* as a kind of spiritual marriage, which joins a person in union with one's "life hid with Christ in God,"[78] that is, the previously unknown part of one's being which connects one with the divine. Still others, he says, "repeat[ed] certain Hebrew words," and he reports the invocations they used (which are actually not Hebrew words)—"Basema, Chamosse, Baonara, Mistadia, Ruada, Kousta, Babaphor, Kalacheit"[79]—which allude to the hidden names of God. After the invocations and prayers, those who participated pronounced a blessing ("Peace to all upon whom this name rests"), anointed the initiate with balsam oil, and chanted "Amen." There were others, Irenaeus says, who rejected any kind of ritual at all, for they said that "recognizing [God's] ineffable greatness" *itself* constitutes *redemption*; thus whoever recognized this already had been "set free."[80]

Whatever form the ritual took, the candidate usually was required to answer a set of questions. Just as the sacraments of baptism and marriage involve a ritual dialogue that shows what the person intends and pledges ("Do you believe in God, the Father . . . ?" "Do you take this man/this woman . . . ?"), so those who receive *apolutrosis* were asked questions like these: Who are you? Where do you come from? Where are you going? Many religious groups, including the mystery religions, adapted such a set of standard questions—the kind that a local border patrol might ask travelers—to use in their initiations. We have already seen that the Gospel of Thomas shows Jesus teaching his disciples to respond to questions like these, questions that members of Thomas's circle were probably asked during baptism, or second baptism:

> Jesus said, "If they say to you, '*Where do you come from?*' Say, 'We come from the light; the place where the light [first] came into being . . .' If they say to you, '*Who are you?*' Say, 'We are the children [of the light], and we are the chosen

of the living Father.' If they ask you, 'What is the sign of your Father in you?' Say to them, 'Movement and rest.' "[81]

Those who responded appropriately showed that they knew who they were *spiritually*, and knew how they related to the "living Father" as well as to Jesus, who, like themselves, comes "from the light." Although such teachers practiced *apolutrosis* in many ways, what mattered most to them, Irenaeus says, was that a person experience spiritual rebirth: "They say that it is necessary for those who have received full *gnosis* to be *born again* into the power which is above all things."[82]

But Irenaeus was dismayed at the way such practices were dividing Christians from one another; he declares that "no reform of the church could possibly compensate" for the damage these people were doing as they "cut in pieces and destroy[ed] the great and glorious body of Christ."[83] What *apolutrosis* really means, Irenaeus charges, is not *redemption* at all but something very different—namely, that Satan was inspiring these so-called spiritual teachers to "*deny that baptism is rebirth to God, and to renounce the whole faith.*"[84] By devaluing what they held in common with other believers and initiating people into their own smaller groups, such teachers were creating potentially innumerable schisms throughout Christian groups worldwide, as well as in each congregation. Irenaeus concludes by declaring that any spiritual teachers or prophets who do these things are actually heretics, frauds, and liars. He writes his massive, five-volume attack, *The Refutation and Overthrow of Falsely So-Called Knowledge*, to demand that members of his congregation stop listening to any of them and return to the basic foundation of their faith. Irenaeus promises that he will explain for them what the Scriptures really mean and insists that only what he teaches is true.

His primary challenge was this: How could he persuade believers that the "common" baptism, which all believers receive, far from being merely the preliminary step in the life of faith, actually effects, as he claims, "rebirth to God"? And how could he persuade them that it conveys not just the elementary teaching that beginners need but nothing less than the "whole faith"? In response, Irenaeus helped construct the basic architecture of what would become orthodox Christianity. His instructions to congregations about which revelations to destroy and which ones to keep—and, perhaps even more important, how to interpret those they kept—would become the basis for the formation of the New Testament and what he calls its "canon of truth," which, in turn, would become the framework for the orthodox creeds. None of these, of course, were Irenaeus's single-handed accomplishment; on the contrary, as he was the first to point out, he built upon what he loved to call "apostolic tradition" and incorporated the efforts of many others. This does mean, however, that the actions he took, developed by his ecclesiastical successors, proved decisive for what would become Christianity as we know it—as well as what we would not know of it—for millennia to come.

ʇoʇoʇoʇ

CONSTANTINE AND THE CATHOLIC CHURCH

When I found that I no longer believed everything I thought Christians were supposed to believe, I asked myself, Why not just leave Christianity—and religion—behind, as so many others have done? Yet I sometimes encountered, in churches and elsewhere—in the presence of a venerable Buddhist monk, in the cantor's singing at a bar mitzvah, and on mountain hikes—something compelling, powerful, even terrifying that I could not ignore, and I had come to see that, besides *belief,* Christianity involves *practice*—and paths toward transformation.

Last Christmas Eve, I went to the midnight service with my sixteen-year-old daughter, Sarah, who, as an infant, when I carried her with me to the Church of the Heavenly Rest in New York, would raise her head to listen intently to the singing cascading down from the choir loft. When she was eight, she joined the choir at Trinity, a Protestant church in Princeton, because, she said, "the music helps my heart." Now, eight years later, after walking in the cold, we slowly pressed our way through the crowded church and found a place to sit close together on the stone stairs behind the lectern, where the choir was standing. This celebration was one that I loved as a child, and had come to love again as an adult, especially since the birth of our first child, Mark, and later of Sarah and David. Since Mark's death, however, I had found participation difficult.

But this year I found myself wholeheartedly singing the carols and listening to the stories of the child born in Bethlehem, angels breaking through darkness to announce the miraculous birth—stories that most New Testament scholars, knowing that we have little or no historical information about Jesus' birth, regard as a mixture of legend and *midrash*, that is, storytelling that draws upon Israel's stories of the miraculous birth of Isaac, of the prophet Samuel, and of the rescue of the infant Moses. On that night, my own associations with those stories seemed to be embraced in the joy and solemnity of the festival, laced, as it is, with intimations of Jesus' impending death as well as the promise of his continuing radiant presence. Attending to the sounds and the silence, the candlelight and darkness, I felt the celebration take us in and break over us like the sea. When it receded, it left me no longer clinging to particular moments in the past but borne upon waves of love and gratitude that moved me toward Sarah, toward the whole community gathered there, at home, or everywhere, the dead and the living. For a moment I was shocked by the thought: We could have made all this up out of what had happened in our own lives; but, of course, we did not *have to* do that, for, as I realized at once, countless *other* people have already done that, and have woven the stories of innumerable lives into the stories and music, the meanings and visions of Jesus' birth. Thus such celebrations are borne along through all the generations that have shaped and re-shaped them, and those that continue to do so, just as encountering the tradition may shape and reshape us.

Many Christians today, however, might ask the same question Irenaeus asked: If spiritual understanding may arise from human experience, doesn't this mean that it is nothing but human invention—and therefore false? According to Irenaeus, it is heresy to assume that human experience is analogous to divine reality, and to infer that each one of us, by exploring our own experience, may discover intimations of truth about God. So, he says, when Valentinus and his disciples opened John's gospel and wanted to understand what *word* means, they reflected on how *word* functions in human experience.[1] What this means, he says, is that they mistook their own projections for theology, so that they found in the Scriptures only what they invented, "each one seeking to validate his own experience."[2] But Irenaeus himself believed that, on the contrary, whatever we might say about our own experience has nothing to do with God:

> So it is that heaping together with a kind of plausibility all human emotions, mental exercises, and formation of in-tentions, and utterances of words, *they have lied with no plau-sibility at all against God. For they ascribe the things that happen to human beings, and whatever they recognize themselves as experienc-ing, to the divine word.*[3]

Had those heretics been right, Irenaeus continues, we would have no need of revelation; "the coming of the Lord will appear unnecessary and useless, if, indeed, he did come intending to tolerate and preserve each person's ideas concerning God."

What Irenaeus objected to was the refusal of those he calls heretics to acknowledge how utterly unique Jesus is, and thus their tendency to place him with ourselves on the human side of the equation. Irenaeus proclaims the opposite: that God—and Jesus Christ, God's manifestation on earth—wholly transcends human modes of thought and experience. Against those who emphasize our kinship with Jesus Christ, Irenaeus argues that Jesus' transcendence sets him apart from the rest of humanity:

> I have shown from the scriptures that *no one of all the sons of Adam is, in his own right, called "God" or named "Lord."* But that *He is himself, and in his own right . . . beyond all men who ever lived, God, and Lord, and Eternal King, and Only-begotten, and Incarnate Logos,* is proclaimed by all the prophets, the apostles, and by the Spirit itself, [and] may be seen by all who have attained to even a modicum of truth.[4]

Furthermore, he adds, "those who say that [Jesus] was merely a human being, begotten by Joseph" show themselves ungrateful to the *"word* of God, who *became flesh* [John 1:14] for them."[5] Not only was Jesus' birth—his "spiritual generation from God"—completely different from ordinary human birth but so was his death completely different from ours. For just as he alone was born miraculously from a virgin, so he alone, of the whole

human race, having died, rose bodily from the dead—"rose in the substance of flesh, and *pointed out to his disciples the mark of the nails and the wound in his side.*"[6]

Nevertheless Irenaeus had to respond to a question that many people—Jews as well as "heretics"—apparently asked him: What is *wrong* with seeing Jesus as if he were simply "one of us"? Haven't we all—ourselves as well as he—been created in the image of God? Irenaeus agrees but adds that the original affinity between God and ourselves was obliterated when the human race surrendered to the power of evil. "Although by nature we belonged to the all-powerful God," he explains, the devil, whom he calls "the apostasy," captured and came to dominate the human race and "alienated us [from God], contrary to nature, and made us his own."[7] Thus we were all in a desperate situation and would have been utterly destroyed had not the divine *word* descended from heaven to save us; for "there is no other way we could have learned about God unless our Master, existing as the word, had become man"[8] and shed his blood to redeem us from the evil one.

How, then, could Irenaeus safeguard this essential gospel message—upon which he believed salvation depends? As we have seen, when Irenaeus confronted the challenge of the many spiritual teachers, he acted decisively, by demanding that believers destroy all those "innumerable secret and illegitimate writings"[9] that his opponents were always invoking, and by declaring that, of all versions of the "gospel" circulating among Christians, only four are genuine. In taking these two momentous—and, as it turned out, enormously influential—steps, Irenaeus became a chief architect of what Christians in later generations called the

New Testament *canon*, a carpenter's term meaning "guideline"—often a string with a weight attached—to check that a wall is straight.[10]

Yet Irenaeus himself never applied the term *canon*, as we do, to the collection of writings he called the "four formed gospel," nor to any other list of writings, since he knew that lists of writings don't prevent heresy. After all, Valentinus and his followers often drew their inspiration from the same sources that most Christians revered in common, including Genesis, Paul's letters, and the gospels of Matthew and Luke. Thus Irenaeus was determined to establish an even more authoritative "canon": it was to be a guideline for understanding any writing or preaching—any gospel at all.

Since both he and his opponents started with the "canon of faith received in baptism,"[11] how could Irenaeus make sure that all believers would take this to mean what he believed it meant—that Jesus is God incarnate? To do so, he declares that he will prove the heretics wrong by using their own favorite gospel against them. He intends to establish what he calls the "canon of truth," and to produce from his own reading of John—by reformulating the baptismal teaching in language he borrows from that gospel—language that his successors would build into the Nicene Creed, and the creeds that followed. But how did John's teaching that Jesus is God's word in human form become what Irenaeus wanted to make it: the very touchstone of orthodoxy?

This question would be easier to answer if the meaning of John's gospel were obvious. But we have seen how controversial it was among its earliest readers: Irenaeus complains that Valentinus's disciples were "always quoting the Gospel of John,"[12] while, surprisingly, prominent "fathers of the church," including three of his revered mentors, apparently were not.[13] Irenaeus probably was aware that his own teacher, Bishop Polycarp of Smyrna, may not have known John's gospel; at any rate, he chose not to mention it, so far as we know. Nor is John's gospel mentioned by another martyr Irenaeus revered, Ignatius, bishop of nearby Antioch,[14] nor, for that matter, by Justin Martyr, the Christian philosopher in Rome whose works Irenaeus also admired. He does mention that some Christians, including some who opposed the "new prophecy" movement, rejected John's gospel. Perhaps he knew that the Roman teacher Gaius had called the Gospel of John heretical[15] and charged that it was actually written not by Jesus' disciple but by John's worst enemy, the heretic Cerinthus.[16] Irenaeus was not, however, the first to introduce this gospel into circles of "ecclesiastical" Christians; some years earlier, another of Justin's students, the Syrian Tatian, had included it with several others, including Matthew and Luke, when he rewrote these accounts and other sources into his own composite "gospel"; and the many fragments that remain of Tatian's long version show that it was widely read.[17] Irenaeus himself treats the Gospel of John as part of the tradition he received from his home community in Asia Minor; but while he champions this gospel, and repeats the tradition that "John, the disciple of the Lord,"[18] wrote it while he lived in Ephesus, he must have known that many Christians found it problematic, even suspect.

Why, then, did Irenaeus join the Gospel of John with the three much more widely accepted gospels of Matthew, Mark, and Luke, and claim it was an indispensable element of the four formed gospel?[19] And why did he place John not, as Christians did later, as the *fourth* gospel but instead as the *first and foremost* pillar of "the church's gospel"? Irenaeus says that the gospel deserves this exalted position because John—and John alone—proclaims Christ's *divine* origin, that is, his

> original, powerful and glorious generation from the Father, thus declaring, *"In the beginning was the word, and the word was with God, and the word was God* [John 1:1–2]." Also, *"all things were made through him* [*the word*] *and without him nothing was made* [John 1:3]."[20]

Irenaeus tells us that Valentinus's disciple Ptolemy, reading these words, envisioned God, *word,* and finally Jesus Christ as, so to speak, waves of divine energy flowing down from above; thus, he suggests, the infinite divine Source above reveals itself in diminished form in the divine *word,* which reveals itself, in turn, in the more limited form of the human Jesus.[21] But Irenaeus declares that such an interpretation misses what we saw in Chapter 2 as the central conviction John wants to convey—that Jesus embodies the divine *word* that comes forth from God and so, on earth, is "Lord and God" to those who recognize him. So Irenaeus challenges Ptolemy's interpretation of John's prologue and argues instead that "God the Father" is equivalent to the *word,* and the *word* is equivalent to "Jesus Christ." He states emphatically that John means there is

> One God all powerful and one Jesus Christ, "through whom all things came into being" [John 1:3]; he says, the *same one* "Son of God" [1:14]; the *same one* "only begotten" [1:14, 18]; the *same one* "Maker of all things"; the *same one*

"true light enlightening everyone" [1:9], the *same one* creator of "all things" [1:3], the *same one* "coming to his own" [1:11]; the *same one* that "became flesh, and dwelt among us" [1:14]."[22]

What Irenaeus's successors would derive from this was a kind of simple, almost mathematical equation, in which God = word = Jesus Christ.[23] That many Christians to this day consider some version of this equation the essence of Christian belief is a mark of Irenaeus's accomplishment—and his success. Irenaeus wants to emphasize this point when he repeats that Jesus Christ *himself* manifests the "one God almighty" who is the "Maker of the universe." And because Irenaeus's bold interpretation came virtually to define orthodoxy, those who read John's gospel today in any language except the Greek original will find that the translations make his conclusion seem obvious—namely, that the man "who dwelt among us" was God incarnate (for discussion of the Greek original, see endnote).[24]

This, then, is the "canon of truth" which Irenaeus reformulates in language he borrows from John's prologue: that "there is one all-powerful God, who made all things by his word. . . . So the scripture says, 'all things were made through him and without him nothing was made' [John 1:3]."[25] Instead of envisioning God on high remote from this world, especially from its deficiencies and sufferings, Irenaeus declares that God manifests himself in and through this world, even choosing to inhabit it himself, as Jesus Christ, the "word made flesh."

Irenaeus argues that this "canon of truth" enables him—and anyone else who uses it—to read not only the gospels but all Scripture in the radical way pioneered by some of his Christian predecessors. Wherever the Jewish Scriptures mention God's *word*, or even where they mention the *Lord God* himself, Irenaeus now claims to find *Jesus Christ*. So, he argues, when God *spoke* to Abraham, it was "our Lord, the *word* of God, who spoke"—not only to Abraham but to all the patriarchs and prophets:

> No doubt . . . the Son of God is implanted everywhere throughout his Scriptures; at one time speaking with Abraham; at another time, with Noah, giving him the dimensions of the ark . . . at another time, he directs Jacob on his journey, and speaks with Moses from the burning bush.[26]

When the prophet Ezekiel saw the Lord surrounded by angels and worshiped in heaven, Irenaeus declares that the One he saw on the throne was *Jesus Christ*.[27] Even when Genesis tells how "the Lord took clay from the earth, and formed *adam*" (Genesis 2:7), Irenaeus declares that "the Lord God" who created humankind in Paradise was "our Lord Jesus Christ, who 'was made flesh' [John 1:14] and was hung upon the cross."[28]

Irenaeus knew that this claim far oversteps anything found in the Gospels of Matthew, Mark, and Luke, where, he notes, each pictures Jesus as a man who receives special divine power, as God's "anointed one." Each of these gospel writers assigns Jesus a somewhat different—human—role. Thus, Irenaeus says, Matthew depicts Jesus as God's appointed king and traces his family back to King David;[29] Luke emphasizes his role as priest;[30] and Mark depicts him primarily as God's prophet.[31] But each of these gospels stops short of identifying Jesus with God, much less *as* God. For Irenaeus, however, the Gospel of John does precisely that; as the church father Origen said later, only John speaks of Jesus' "divinity." Irenaeus, like Origen, took this to mean that John is not only different but also "more elevated," having seen what the others missed; and from this conviction he apparently concluded that only by joining John with the others could the church complete the "fourfold gospel," which teaches that Jesus is God incarnate. Carried away with enthusiasm, Irenaeus identifies personally with the evangelist and declares that "John, the Lord's disciple," wrote this gospel for precisely the same purpose that he himself now was writing his *own* book— namely, to expose "heretics"; to confound those who spread "falsely so-called *gnosis*"; and, above all, "to establish the *canon of truth* in the church."[32]

Having set forth his reformulated *canon of truth*—that God the Father is also the Creator who "made all things through his word" (John 1:3), the *word* that became incarnate in Jesus Christ— Irenaeus turns to the practical question: Who worships God rightly, and who does not? First, he says, the Jews do not, since they refuse to see that "the word of the Lord" which spoke to Abraham and Moses was none other than Jesus Christ. Because they do not identify "the word of the Lord" as Jesus Christ, Irenaeus declares,

> the Jews have departed from God, *since they have not received his word,* but they imagined that they could know the Father . . . without the word, *being ignorant of the God who spoke in human form* to Abraham and then to Moses.[33]

Since they fail to recognize Jesus as "the God who spoke in human form" to their ancestors, Irenaeus says that God disinherited the Jews and stripped them of their right to be his priests. Although they continue to worship, God rejects their offerings as he rejected Cain's, since, just as Cain killed Abel, so the Jews "killed the Just One," Jesus, so that "their hands are full of blood."[34]

Thus the Jews worship God in vain, for he has transferred their priesthood to those who *did* recognize his "word"[35]—namely, the apostles whom Jesus taught to offer "the sacrifice of the new covenant," when he told them to offer the bread he called his body and the wine he called his blood. Ever since Jesus' death on the cross, the eucharist that reenacts his sacrifice is the lightning rod that draws God's power down to earth. Not only does the eucharist alone offer access to God but, Irenaeus declares, "this pure sacrifice *only the church offers—not the Jews . . . nor any of the assemblies of the heretics.*"[36]

Since Irenaeus assumed—rightly, no doubt—that few Jews would read what he wrote, much less contest his claim that God rejects their worship, he spent little time arguing that they are excluded. But he did anticipate objections he expected members of his Christian audience to raise: Isn't the eucharist a holy sacrifice when *any* baptized Christian—or, at least, any priest—offers it as Jesus taught his disciples to do? Irenaeus says no: when heretics offer the eucharist, they do so in vain. For those who accept his canon of truth, what matters is not only to be a *Christian* but to be an *orthodox* Christian—that is, one who "thinks straight."

Instead of asserting his own authority to interpret the gospel against that of his opponents, Irenaeus identifies his own belief with that of the whole consensus of what he calls "apostolic tradition." Thus, he insists, "orthodox" Christians are those who uphold the fourfold gospel *together with* the canon of truth—

later to be expanded into the great creeds—that directs how to interpret it. I do not mean to suggest that he set out to deceive his audience. On the contrary, Irenaeus surely shared the conviction that made "orthodox Christianity" so compelling to him, as well as to many other Christians to this day: that "the faithful," as trustworthy stewards, hand down only what they, in turn, received from the apostles, without adding or subtracting anything from what Irenaeus and others call the *depositum fidei*—the faith that the apostles deposited, as in a bank. By invoking the authority of the ancient consensus of the apostles they can claim, then, that what they teach is not only the *unchanging truth* but absolutely *certain*.[37]

Irenaeus warns that eternal salvation depends on discriminating between which priests in Christian churches are "genuine" and which are, in his words, "heretics, schismatics, or hypocrites," and he calls on believers to *obey* the former and *shun* the latter:

> Therefore it is necessary to *obey the priests who are in the church*—those who have received the succession from the apostles, as we have shown, and who have also received. . . . the *certain gift of truth* . . . *but to hold in suspicion those who stand apart from the primary line of succession, and who gather in any place whatsoever, [and to regard them] either as heretics with evil intentions or as schismatics, puffed up with themselves, or as hypocrites.*[38]

Irenaeus knew that the "disciples of Valentinus" did not oppose the clergy. On the contrary, what made them especially hard for him to discredit was the fact that many of them were priests themselves. Yet he warns believers to beware of those whose claims to priestly office are virtually identical to any others' but who actually are *heretics* who "serve only themselves," and not God. He says that believers must be careful to associate only with priests who worship God *rightly.* This means not only that they "teach sound doctrines" but that they speak "sound words" and display "blameless conduct"—in short, they do not hold unauthorized meetings, or claim access to secret teaching, or perform special initiations.

Irenaeus ends his five-volume *Refutation* calling upon his fellow believers to judge and excommunicate heretics. Recalling how God's wrath falls upon the Jews "who became the killers of their Lord," he declares that truly spiritual Christians must also condemn "all the followers of Valentinus," since, although many believers see them as fellow Christians, they actually subvert the faith and, like the Jews, have become "sons of the devil." Finally he contrasts those who take "many deviant paths" with those who "belong to the church," who share

> one and the same faith, observe the same precepts, and . . .
> protect the same form of ecclesiastical constitution . . . in
> which one and the same path of salvation is demonstrated
> throughout the world.[39]

Vividly evoking the final judgment pictured in the Revelation, he leaves the reader with visions of the devil, the antichrist, and all their demonic powers being cast into eternal fire along with all of their human offspring, while the heavenly Jerusalem descends to welcome "the priests and the disciples of the apostles" along with "the faithful."[40] For Irenaeus, then, and for his successors, *making a difference* between true Christians and those

he calls heretics—and choosing the path of "orthodox" faith
and practice—is what ultimately makes the difference between
heaven and hell.

We do not know how members of Irenaeus's own congregation reacted to his pleas, although we *do* know how distressed
he was that the great majority of Christians initially accepted
the Valentinians' view of themselves. While Irenaeus, as bishop,
was working to expose them as "wolves in sheeps' clothing"[41]
and expel them from the churches, he wrote that most Christians regarded them as among their most influential and advanced members. In his own time, Valentinus had been widely
respected as a teacher by his fellow Christians in Rome,[42] and
even a generation later Irenaeus's contemporary the famous
Egyptian teacher Clement of Alexandria, as well as Clement's
brilliant successor, Origen, engaged in discussion and argument
with prominent disciples of Valentinus, and regarded them as
fellow Christian teachers. Although Clement and Origen often
criticized aspects of Valentinian theology, they also adopted elements of it into their own teaching.[43]

About twenty years after Irenaeus wrote, Tertullian described
how his fellow believers in Carthage reacted when he warned
them against joining circles he called heretical:

> "How does it happen," they ask, "that this woman or that
> man, who were *the most faithful, the most circumspect, and the*
> *most respected in the church,* have gone over to the other
> side?"[44]

But Irenaeus was convinced that the presence of the Valentinian Christians was dangerously divisive—that it undermined

the preaching of the gospel and the authority of its leaders. He wanted them either to abandon their "heresy" or be cut off from the churches. We do not know how his contemporaries responded; I would guess that the majority, moved by his concern, rallied around Irenaeus and, rather than risk expulsion, chose the safer shelter of the church community and what Irenaeus insisted was the stable authority of the "catholic" consensus of churches and their clergy. In any case, we know that Christians in later generations increasingly followed his lead, as many tried to compel those who persisted in "heresy" either to conform or to separate themselves from the churches. For during the following century and a half, as rapidly growing numbers of converts joined Christian churches despite sporadic outbursts of violent persecution, many bishops adopted and developed the safeguards Irenaeus had outlined to strengthen what he had called the "same form of ecclesiastical constitution" by standardizing basic Christian instruction and excluding those who deviated from the "one . . . path of salvation." During the fourth century, when persecution suddenly gave way to official toleration of Christians under Constantine, and then to the construction of a Christian empire, a coalition of bishops would take up Irenaeus's agenda and attempt to realize his vision of a catholic—that is, universal—orthodox church.

During Irenaeus's lifetime, of course, this astonishing turn of events lay a hundred and fifty years in the future. As we have seen, his Valentinian opponents had never intended to go their own separate way. But many of them rejected the alternatives Irenaeus placed before them: either accept the common faith as "the whole faith" or reject it entirely. Instead, they continued to affirm the common faith as a first step toward truth but questioned not only what it means but what lies beyond it. Among themselves they not only recognized diversity but expected and welcomed it, as philosophers did in their discussions, as evidence of original and creative insight.[45] So, Tertullian wrote caustically,

When they consider that "spiritual seed in everyone," whenever they hit upon something new, they immediately call their audacity a spiritual gift—no unity, only diversity! And so we see clearly that most of them disagree with one another, since they are willing to say—and even sincerely—of certain points, "This is not so," and "I take this to mean something different," and "I do not accept that."[46]

Tertullian expressed shock, too, that, as in some philosophic circles, women participated with men: "These heretical women— how audacious they are! They are bold enough to teach, to preach, to take part in almost every masculine function—they may even baptize people!"[47] While they appreciated diverse viewpoints within their own circles, such Christians may have extended less tolerance and generosity toward the "simple" believers who followed the bishop. Irenaeus wrote that when he directly questioned Valentinians and challenged them, they either remained silent or said that he was simply wrong, since he had not yet advanced beyond a naïve level of understanding.[48]

Irenaeus, for his part, says that when these "absolutely foolish and stupid people" were threatened with excommunication, they sometimes replied that they no longer believed in the God whom he invoked as an angry judge ready to cast unbelievers into the fires of hell. Moreover, they questioned his understanding of the Scriptures. Some asked, for example, how one could worship a God who first "hardened the heart of Pharaoh and his servants"[49] and then punished them by drowning them in the sea. Or how could a just God *refrain* from condemning Lot for impregnating his own daughters when he was drunk?[50] As we have seen, the author of the Gospel of Truth says that those who come to know the infinite goodness and compassion that belong to "the fullness of God" no longer think of God in terms of such deficient and anthropomorphic images.

Others, including Valentinus's disciple Heracleon, interpreted disparity between Christians in terms not unlike what the psychologist William James would call "varieties of religious experience."[51] Heracleon contrasts two qualitatively different types of conversion experience. He says that the great majority of Christians appeal to God only when they are desperate, and turn to faith only when they see miracles; thus the gospels often depict Jesus as a wonder-worker who heals the sick, raises the dead, and walks on water. Since they experience the human situation—their own situation—as pervaded by suffering and threatened by death, these Christians see Jesus above all as a healer and savior. Heracleon says that John characterizes this kind of conversion when he tells how Jesus, traveling to Galilee, met a ruler who begged him to come down and heal his son, who was desperately ill. Although Jesus rebuked him for the deficiency of his faith ("Unless you see signs and wonders, you will not believe"), the ruler renewed his pleas: "Sir, come down before my child dies." But after Jesus challenged him to have faith ("Go: your son will live") and his son recovered, the story concludes that "he himself believed, and all his household."[52]

This type of conversion experience, Heracleon says, is familiar to those Christians who see God as John pictures this ruler—as a strict, limited, but well-meaning master and father, who has decreed the death penalty for every one of his children who sins and yet loves them and grieves when they perish. But they also believe that, apart from Jesus' sacrificial death on the cross, God does not forgive his own children; he actually saves only those who "believe."

One might ask, how *else* could one see God than as divine ruler, father, and judge? And how else could one see Jesus, except as a miracle worker and savior? Isn't that how the gospels depict him? Heracleon says that John tells the story of the "woman at the well" to show, by contrast, how a person gifted with grace experiences conversion. Here John recounts how Jesus, tired from travel, sits down to rest near a well, asks a Samaritan woman who comes to draw water to give him a drink, and offers her, in return, "living water":

> The woman said to him, "Sir, you have nothing to draw with, and the well is deep; where do you get that living water?" . . . Jesus said to her, *"Whoever drinks from this water will thirst again, but whoever drinks from the water that I shall give him will never thirst; the water that I give will become in him a spring of water, welling up to eternal life."*
>
> *The woman said to him, "Sir, give me this water, so that I may not be thirsty, nor come here to draw." Jesus said, "Go, call your husband, and come here." . . .* Jesus said to her, *"Woman, believe me, the*

hour is coming . . . and is now, when the true worshipers will worship
the father in spirit and in truth. . . . God is spirit, and those who wor-
ship him must worship in spirit and truth."[53]

Heracleon explains that for John, as for the prophet Isaiah, *water*
means "spiritual nourishment"; thus, the story shows that the
woman is aware of spiritual thirst and, not knowing how to sat-
isfy it, she has come to draw water from the "well of Jacob,"
which signifies traditional ways of worshiping God. But since
these leave her thirst unsatisfied, when Jesus offers to reveal the
source of a wellspring within herself, she immediately grasps
what he means and responds, "Give me this water!"

Heracleon points out that Jesus' answer ("Go, call your husband, and come here")[54] makes no sense: not only does he not
respond to her request but, as the story shows, he knows that
she is not married. Bewildered by his words, the woman initially takes them literally and admits that she is unmarried but
has lived with six men. Heracleon says that Jesus reveals to her
that she has lived this way "through ignorance of God and the
needs of her own life."[55] When he tells her to "call her husband,"
he is showing her that she already has a "partner" in divine
being—that is, a relationship to God of which she is not yet
aware. He directs her to call upon resources she already has
been given, and to discover her spiritual counterpart, her "fulfillment" (*pleroma* in Greek). Once she recognizes this as an essential part of her being, she may celebrate communion with
God as the divine "marriage."

Different as these two types of conversion experience are,
they are by no means mutually exclusive. The first sees salvation as deliverance from sin and death; the second shows how

someone "ignorant of God and of [one's] own nature," and mired in destructive activity, eventually develops a growing awareness of—and need for—relationship with God. Heracleon explains that whoever experiences the first type of conversion may—eventually will—also experience the second, which is what Augustine, writing two centuries later, meant when he spoke of "faith seeking understanding."

Heracleon explains that most Christians tend to take literally the images they find in the Scriptures: they see God as the *creator* who made this present world, the *lawgiver* who gave tablets to Moses on Sinai, the divine *father* who begot Jesus. But those who experience God's presence come to see these traditional images of God for what they are—human creations. One need not *reject* such images, Heracleon says, since they provide an essential way of pointing toward divine reality that words cannot express; but one may come to see that all religious language—and much other language—consists of such images. Whoever realizes this comes to worship God, as Jesus says, "in spirit and in truth."[56]

While Irenaeus sought to clarify basic convictions about God and Jesus Christ in theological statements that would become the framework of the fourth-century creeds, Valentinian Christians accorded such theological propositions a much less important role. Instead of regarding these as the essential and certain basis for spiritual understanding—and instead of rejecting them—they treated them as elementary teachings and emphasized instead what Irenaeus mentions only in passing—how far God surpasses human comprehension.

The Secret Book of John, similarly, sets forth what theologians call the *via negativa*, recognizing what *cannot* be known and

discarding misapprehensions about God. Nevertheless, the Secret Book says that human beings have an innate capacity to
know God but one that offers only hints and glimpses of divine
reality.[57] The Secret Book suggests that the story of Eve's birth
from Adam's side speaks of the awakening of this spiritual capacity. Instead of simply telling about the origin of woman, this
story, symbolically read, shows how the "blessed one above, the
Father" (or, in some versions of the text, the "Mother-Father"),
feeling compassion for Adam, sent him

> a "helper"—luminous *epinoia* ["creative" or "inventive"
> consciousness] which comes out of him, who is called Life
> [Eve]; and she "helps" the whole creation, by working with
> him, and by restoring him to his full being, and by teach-
> ing him about the descent of his kind, and by showing the
> way to ascend, the way he came down.[58]

Thus Eve symbolizes the gift of spiritual understanding, which
enables us to reflect—however imperfectly—upon divine reality.
Another book discovered at Nag Hammadi, On the Origin of
the World, says that when the first man and woman recognized
their nakedness, "they saw that they were naked of spiritual understanding [*gnosis*]." But then the luminous *epinoia* "appeared to
them shining with light, and awakened their consciousness."[59]

The Secret Book intends this story to show that we have a la-
tent capacity within our hearts and minds that links us to the
divine—not in our ordinary state of mind but when this hidden capacity awakens. Because the term *epinoia* has no precise
equivalent in English, I shall leave it in Greek. To speak of various modes of consciousness susceptible to revelation, the au-

thor of the Secret Book invokes a cluster of words related to the Greek verb *noein*, which means "perceive," "think," or "be aware." The Secret Book explains that, although God is essentially incomprehensible, the powers that reveal God to humankind include *pronoia* (anticipatory awareness), *ennoia* (internal reflection), and *prognosis* (foreknowledge or intuition), all personified as feminine presences, presumably because of the gender of the Greek words. But according to the Secret Book it is, above all, the "luminous *epinoia*" that conveys genuine insight. We might translate this as "imagination," but many people take this term as Irenaeus did, to refer to fantasy rather than conscious awareness. Yet as the Secret Book envisions it, *epinoia* (and related modes of awareness) remains an ambiguous, limited—but indispensable— gift. When John asks whether everyone receives the luminous *epinoia*, the savior answers yes—"The power will descend *upon every person*, for without it, no one can stand"—[60] and adds that *epinoia* strengthens those who love her by enabling them to discriminate between good and evil, so that moral insight and ethical power are inseparable from spiritual understanding: "When the spirit of life increases, and the power comes and strengthens that soul, no one can any longer deceive it with works of evil."[61]

The author of the Secret Book stresses that the insights this spiritual intuition conveys are neither complete nor certain; instead, *epinoia* conveys hints and glimpses, images and stories, that imperfectly point beyond themselves toward what we cannot now fully understand. Thus the author knows that these very stories—those told in the Secret Book—are to be taken neither literally nor too seriously; for these, too, are merely glimpses that, as Paul says, we now know only "in a mirror, darkly."[62] Yet, however incomplete, these glimpses suffice to reveal the presence of the divine, for the Secret Book says that, apart from spiritual intuition, "people grow old without joy . . . and die . . . without knowing God."[63]

How is it, then, that many people remain oblivious to *epinoia*? To answer this question, the Secret Book tells a story intended to show that although the creator-god pictured in Genesis is *himself* only an anthropomorphic image of the divine Source that brought forth the universe, many people mistake this deficient image for God. This story tells how the creator-god himself, being unaware of the "blessed one, the Mother-Father, the blessed and compassionate One" above, boasted that he was the only God ("I am a jealous God; there is none other besides me").[64] Intent on maintaining sole power, he tried to control his human creatures by forbidding them to eat the fruit of the tree of knowledge. But when Adam and Eve disobeyed him, and chose to seek knowledge of the divine Source above, he realized that they had listened to their inner resource, the luminous *epinoia*. As soon as the creator-god realized what they had done, he retaliated; first he punished them both, and even cursed the earth itself because of them;[65] then he tried to force the woman to subject herself to the man, saying, "Your husband shall rule over you";[66] and, finally, "all his angels cast them out of Paradise,"[67] burdening them with "bitter fate" and with daily cares to make them oblivious to the "luminous *epinoia*."[68]

But this is a mythical explanation. Can we find a more practical reason for the suppression of the "luminous *epinoia*"? I suggest that the author of the Secret Book knew how Christians like Irenaeus challenged those who spoke of the "God beyond God," and insisted that everyone worship only the creator. But while Valentinus's followers often met such challenges with silence, the author of the Secret Book returns the challenge in stories such as this one that are meant to show how—and why—such leaders, in the name of the God they serve, consign spiritual Christians to hell. The Secret Book suggests that those who worship God only as creator—including most Christians—share his animosity toward spiritual awareness, and also toward those who speak for its presence in human experience. The story of the creator's hostility to *epinoia*, then, is a parable, both comic and painful, of conflict between those who seek spiritual intuition and those who suppress it.

Irenaeus, shocked and distressed by such readings of Genesis, protests that his opponents place far too little confidence in traditional sources of revelation—and far too much in their own imagination:

> *To what distance above God do you lift up your imaginations, you rash and inflated people?* . . . God cannot be measured in the heart, and in the mind he is incomprehensible—he who holds the earth in the hollow of his hand. Who knows the measure of his right hand? Who knows his finger? Or do you understand his hand—that hand which measures immensity? For his hand lays hold of all things, and illumines the heavens, and also the things below the heavens, and tests the reins and the hearts, and is present in mysteries and in our secret thoughts, and does openly nourish and sustain us. . . . Yet, *as if now they had measured and thoroughly investigated him . . . they pretend that beyond [God] there is . . . another Father—certainly they are not looking up to heavenly things, as they claim, but really descending into a profound abyss of insanity.*[69]

But it would take more than theological argument for Irenaeus's viewpoint to prevail in churches throughout the world: it would take, in fact, the revolution initiated by the Roman emperor Constantine. In his famous *History of the Church*, Eusebius of Caesarea, a bishop in Palestine who survived years of persecution in which many of his friends and fellow Christians died, wrote how God miraculously intervened on October 28, 312, by revealing Christ's sign in the heavens to the pagan emperor Constantine and gaining his allegiance.[70] Eusebius then tells how, in the years that followed, Constantine declared amnesty for Christians and became their imperial patron. But this practical military leader chose to recognize only those who belonged to what may have become, by his time, the best-organized and largest group, which he called the "lawful and most holy catholic church."[71]

Constantine's recognition carried with it, of course, enormous benefits. In 313 the emperor ordered that anyone who had confiscated property from "the catholic church of the Christians in any city, or even in other places," during the persecutions of the previous decades must return it immediately to "these same churches"[72] and offer compensation for any damages. Eusebius of Caesarea marveled that in this astonishing new era "bishops constantly received even personal letters from the emperor, and honors, and gifts of money."[73] Eusebius includes in his history a letter Constantine wrote the same year to the proconsul of Africa to say that he was exempting Christian clergy from financial obligations incumbent on ordinary citizens; but, since he knew that the African churches were divided into rival factions, he specified that these privileges applied only to those he called the "ministers of the lawful and most holy catholic religion."[74] The emperor also offered tax relief and, later, tax exemptions to clergy who qualified—while threatening to increase taxes for anyone guilty of founding "heretical" churches. About ten years later, apparently responding to what he considered abuses of these privileges, he wrote a new order to specify that

> the privileges that have been granted in consideration of religion *must benefit only the adherents of the catholic faith* [or "law"]. It is Our will, furthermore, that *heretics and schismatics shall not only be alien from these privileges but also shall be bound and subjected to various compulsory public services.*[75]

Besides allocating money to repair damaged churches, Constantine ordered new ones to be built, including, tradition says, a magnificent Church of St. Peter on the Vatican hill in Rome[76] and the Church of the Holy Sepulcher in Jerusalem. In 324 he wrote to the eastern bishops, urging them to "ask without hesitation whatever [funds] you find to be necessary"[77] from the imperial treasury. He assured them that he had already ordered his finance minister to give them whatever they asked to build new churches and fit them with the splendor appropriate to honor the God of the universe. Constantine also delegated to certain bishops the distribution of the imperial grain supply and other necessities to support people in need, so that they might fulfill Jesus' admonitions to care for the sick, the needy, and the destitute, as well as those who had suffered torture, imprisonment, or exile during the years of persecution.[78] Furthermore, while transforming the status of Christians, Constantine's revolution changed the status of Jews. As Timothy Barnes, one of the foremost contemporary historians of these events, writes, "Constantine translated Christian prejudice against Jews into legal disabilities."[79] He forbade Jews to enter Jerusalem, except on the one day a year they were to mourn for having lost it, and ordered them not to seek or accept converts to Judaism. Moreover, Constantine "prescribed that any Jew who attempted forcibly to prevent conversion from Judaism to Christianity should be burned alive."[80]

To strengthen his own alliance with church leaders and to unify fractious Christian groups into one harmonious structure, Constantine charged bishops from churches throughout the empire to meet at his expense at Nicaea, an inland city, near a large lake, to work out a standard formulation of Christian faith. From that meeting and its aftermath, during the tumultuous decades that followed, emerged the Nicene Creed that would effectively clarify and elaborate the "canon of truth," along with what we call the canon—the list of twenty-seven writings which would become the New Testament. Together these would help establish what Irenaeus had envisioned—a worldwide communion of "orthodox" Christians joined into one "catholic and apostolic" church.

How that happened is far more complex than can be related here. I hesitate even to mention the extraordinary events of the fourth century, since no short sketch can adequately describe them; yet I offer one, since these events no doubt are linked to the history we have been exploring. Fortunately, several outstanding historians have written accounts available for the interested reader.[81] For our purposes here, even the briefest summary would have to note how, during the transitional decades after 312, Constantine subjected the Roman empire to a massive restructuring and shifted the underpinnings of imperial power. What he did—and did gradually, in order to minimize opposition from powerful senators—was transfer the empire's basic allegiance from the traditional guardians of its welfare, the gods of Rome, to the foreign god worshiped by those whom his predecessors had persecuted for atheism.[82] It was at this critical time that Constantine convened the international council of bishops to meet at Nicaea, "because of the excellent temperature of the air,"[83] in the early days of June 325. The emperor himself attended the council and participated in it, telling his guests at one of the lavish state dinners that he believed God had appointed him "bishop [the Greek term means "supervisor"] of those outside the church."[84] Although in the past many historians assumed that Constantine directed—even dictated—the entire proceedings, more careful historical investigation has shown that he not only allowed but expected the bishops themselves to arbitrate disputes and to forge a working consensus among rival parties. When he addressed those who gathered at Nicaea, he urged them to resolve their differences "lest private animosities interfere with God's business."[85]

One of the conflicts he hoped to resolve had been troubling churches throughout the empire for several years. As rival Christian groups vied to gain ascendancy in a changed world, the question was no longer *whether* the "catholic church" would prevail against "heretics and schismatics" but *who* would succeed in claiming to embody that catholic church. In Egypt, a group of bishops headed by Alexander, the bishop of Alexandria, and later by his successor Athanasius, took up and extended Irenaeus's agenda. It was he, in fact, who would interpret and update for his contemporaries the "orthodox" side of the controversy earlier engaged in the gospels of Thomas and John. An intense, combative, and single-minded young man, Athanasius, who served as the bishop's secretary, was about eighteen when Alexander engaged in—some would say he started—a conflict that soon divided churches from Egypt to Asia Minor, Syria, and Palestine. Around 318, Alexander had heard that a member of his clergy in Alexandria, a popular Libyan priest named Arius, was preaching that the Word of God, while divine, was not divine in the same way as God the Father. Soon afterward Alexander convened a council of Egyptian bishops to declare Arius's views heretical and excommunicate him, along with all priests and bishops who sided with him, from the church in Alexandria.

This action ignited new controversy. Hearing of Arius's expulsion, bishops in Syria, Palestine, and Asia Minor convened their own councils, several of which declared Arius's teaching not only faithful to catholic tradition but entirely orthodox. Although many bishops urged Alexander to accept Arius back into his church, he adamantly refused. When Alexander and Athanasius received Constantine's summons to Nicaea, to formulate a creed for the "universal" church, they arrived determined to make sure that the carefully chosen—and hotly contested—theological phrases placed there would confess Christ, the Word, as God. They must have been pleased with the result: the formula upon which the majority finally voted, after intense argument, proclaimed that Jesus Christ was "God from God, Light from Light, true God from true God"; that he was "begotten, not made," that is, borrowing John's term, God's "only begotten" offspring (not "made," as were all beings whom God *created*, angels and humans alike).[86]

The next phrase, upon which Alexander and his allies had agreed in advance, proved explosively controversial. To exclude Arius's view that Christ was divine but not in the same sense as God, they insisted on adding that Christ was *"of one being with"*— essentially no different from—God the Father. While the great majority of bishops "were prepared to accept almost any formula that would secure harmony within the church,"[87] those who opposed this phrase pointed out that it occurs neither in the Scriptures nor in Christian tradition. Is it not extreme, they asked, and contrary to the gospels, to say that Jesus Christ is essentially "the same" as God the Father? But those who insisted that he was carried the day; and no doubt it mattered that Constantine, perhaps frustrated by so much time spent wrangling over a phrase, urged the bishops to include it and end the argument. Now that Constantine had endorsed the term, anyone who challenged it might seem to be questioning the orthodoxy of the emperor himself. In any case, all those present signed the document except the few who chose instead to leave: Arius himself, along with some priests and two bishops from Libya who remained loyal to him. Later, however, the inclusion of this phrase intensified controversy among Christians that continued for decades—indeed, for generations (and, some would say, for centuries).

Eventually the Nicene Creed, approved by the bishops and endorsed by Constantine himself, would become the official doctrine that all Christians henceforth must accept in order to participate in the only church recognized by the emperor—the "catholic church." A year before the bishops met at Nicaea, Constantine had tried to legislate an end to "heretical sects," which, by one estimate, may have included about half the Christians in the empire.[88] The emperor ordered all "heretics and schismatics" to stop meeting, even in private houses, and to surrender their churches and whatever property they owned to the catholic church. Although many Christians associated with teachers such as Valentinus, Marcion, and the prophet Montanus ignored the law,[89] and magistrates often failed to enforce it, such legislation lent enormous support to the network of catholic churches.

When Alexander died and Athanasius succeeded him as bishop of Alexandria, Athanasius campaigned tirelessly to induce Christians all over Egypt to unite under this creed, as Irenaeus had envisioned. Constantine's own hopes were more modest; he hoped that the Nicene Creed would offer the basic framework upon which Christians could agree, while allowing room for discussion and disagreement, so long as these did not destroy the fabric of the "universal" church, for, as Barnes observes,

> Constantine believed that all people should be Christian, but that Christians might legitimately hold divergent opinions on theological questions, and that sensible Christians could disagree about doctrine in a spirit of brotherly love.[90]

Some scholars have suggested that these theological disputes were essentially political. The historian Erik Peterson points out that many Christians associated God the Father with the emperor, Jesus Christ with the bishops, and the holy spirit with "the people." Thus, he suggests, Athanasius's claim that the Son is entirely equal with the Father implies that the bishops' authority is equal to that of the emperor himself. Peterson says that this position correlates with Athanasius's refusal to take orders from any emperor, and pervaded the power struggles that characterized the relationship between emperors and bishops in the West throughout the middle ages. Conversely, he says, Arius's formulation, which acknowledges the Father's priority over the Son, survived for centuries in altered form in some of the Eastern churches, which tended to accept imperial power over church affairs, and later would influence the structure of what became "state churches."[91] Whether or not we accept this analysis, we can see that during the decades after the council intense conflict broke out between those who rallied behind Athanasius's position and those who sided with Arius—conflict that engulfed Constantine's sons and grandsons when they succeeded him as emperor and divided bishops and congregations throughout the empire.

As a result, for the next forty years, Athanasius's own position, challenged by those he called Arian Christians—or, as he liked to say, Ariomaniacs—was by no means secure. Although Constantine initially supported Athanasius as Alexander's successor, seven years later he took the side of his opponents and ratified the decision of a council of bishops to depose Athanasius. Forced into exile, Athanasius returned after Constantine's death in 337 to reclaim his position, but two years later he was again deposed by a council of bishops and hid out among his supporters while Bishop Gregory from Cappadocia took over as bishop. Nearly ten years later, when Gregory died, Athanasius returned and reclaimed his office for three more years; but in

349 he was again deposed and replaced by another bishop from Cappadocia. After his third successful rival, having presided as bishop of Alexandria for five years, was lynched in 361, Athanasius succeeded in regaining his position, which he held tenaciously until his death in 373.

Despite such opposition—and perhaps because of it—Athanasius resolved to bring all Egyptian Christians, however diverse, under the supervision of his office. After working to gain the support of ascetic women,[92] he began the more difficult task of establishing his authority over various groups of monks and "holy men," including those who lived in communal monasteries that Pachomius, a former soldier turned monk, had founded throughout Egypt since the legalization of Christianity.[93] In the spring of 367, when Athanasius was in his sixties and more securely established as bishop, he wrote what became his most famous letter. In a world much different from that of Irenaeus, Athanasius included in his annual Easter Letter detailed instructions that would extend and implement the guidelines his predecessor had sketched out nearly two hundred years before. First, he said, since heretics

> have tried to set in order for themselves the so-called apocryphal books and to mix these with the divinely inspired Scripture . . . which those who were eyewitnesses and helpers of the Word handed down to our ancestors, it seemed good to me . . . to set forth in order the canonized and transmitted writings . . . believed to be divine books.[94]

After listing the twenty-two books that he says are "believed to be the Old Testament," Athanasius proceeds to offer the earliest known list of the twenty-seven books he calls the "books of the New Testament," beginning with "the four gospels, Matthew, Mark, Luke, and John," and proceeding to the same list of writings attributed to apostles that constitute the New Testament today. Praising these as the "springs of salvation," he calls upon Christians during this Lenten season to "cleanse the church from every defilement" and to reject "the apocryphal books," which are "filled with myths, empty, and polluted"—books that, he warns, incite conflict and lead people astray. It is likely that one or more of the monks who heard his letter read at their monastery near the town of Nag Hammadi decided to defy Athanasius's order and removed more than fifty books from the monastery library, hid them in a jar to preserve them, and buried them near the cliff where Muḥammad 'Alī would find them sixteen hundred years later.

Although Athanasius intended the "canon of truth," now enshrined in the Nicene Creed, to safeguard "orthodox" interpretation of Scripture, his experience of Christians who disagreed with him showed that these "heretics" could still read the "canonical Scriptures" in ways he considered unorthodox. To prevent such readings, he insists that anyone who reads the Scriptures must do so through *dianoia*—the capacity to discern the *meaning* or *intention* implicit in each text. Above all, he warns believers to shun *epinoia*.[95] What others revere as spiritual intuition Athanasius declares is a deceptive, all-too-human capacity to think subjectively, according to one's preconceptions. *Epinoia* leads only to error—a view that the "catholic church" endorsed then and holds to this day.

Finally, lest anyone seek direct access to God through the "image of God" formed within us in creation, Athanasius took care to block this path as well. In his famous and rhetorically powerful work *On the Incarnation of the Word*, he explains that, although God originally created Adam in his own image, human sin has damaged that image beyond human capacity to repair (a view that Augustine later developed into his understanding of "original sin"). Consequently, there is now only *one* single being who embodies the divine image, and that is the Word of God himself, Jesus Christ:

> Since humankind made in God's image was disappearing, . . . what is the use of humankind originally having been made in God's image? . . . *No one else could re-create the likeness of God's image for human beings except* [*Jesus Christ*], *the Image of the Father.*[96]

While Arius urged believers to emulate Christ, Athanasius declares this effort not only difficult but impossible, even blasphemous: on the contrary, he famously proclaims, "*God became human* so that humankind might become divine." All that a human being can do—*must* do—is believe and receive the salvation that God alone can offer. Thus Athanasius extended what Irenaeus taught: whoever seeks access to God must first have recourse to the Word, whom the believer approaches initially through baptism, by confessing the orthodox faith as contained in the statements of the creed, and by receiving the sacraments—the "medicine of immortality" offered wherever orthodox Christians worship together in church.

Even as a persecuted movement, Christianity had become increasingly visible in cities throughout the empire. During the third and early fourth century, some groups even built their own churches, as the number of converts more than doubled or tripled.[97] Many, no doubt, were persuaded of the truth of Christian faith by the miraculous events that followed Constantine's conversion. No wonder, then, that after 313 many more crowded the churches, not only those seeking some advantage by joining what would become the emperor's church but also, no doubt, others who, although attracted to Christianity, previously had hesitated to receive baptism lest they place themselves and their families in danger. What such converts wanted was not only to share in the promise of divine salvation and eternal life in the next world but also, in this one, to join the "particular Christian society" committed to living according to Christ's precepts—or, at least, according to modified versions of them. Many found in what earlier was a radical alternative to the Roman order a vision of transformed human relationships that now promised to embrace not only home and church but the whole of human society.

This sketch of what happened during the fourth century does not support the simplistic view often expressed by historians in the past—namely, that catholic Christianity prevailed only because it received imperial patronage, or that people participated because their leaders somehow succeeded in coercing them.[98] Several historians have persuasively argued instead that Constantine's decision to affiliate himself with the Christian churches demonstrates the enormous appeal that the Christian movement had held for an increasing numbers of converts long before it was safe to join.[99] Nor does this sketch support the view that Constantine simply used Christianity for cynical purposes.

We do not know his motives, but his actions suggest that he believed he had found in Christ an all-powerful divine patron and the promise of eternal life; and during the thirty years he ruled after that, he legislated, to the extent he considered practical, the moral values he found in biblical sources—the vision of a harmonious society, built upon divine justice, that shows concern even for its poorest members.

Although Constantine's revolution lent support to the claims of catholic bishops that their church, triumphant through God's grace, alone offered salvation, we would be naïve to suppose that Christianity now became, in fact, uniform and homogeneous. Even a glance at the controversies and challenges of the fourth and fifth centuries shows that it did not.[100] What this revolution did accomplish was to enhance the authority of the bishops identified as catholic and to establish their consensus, expressed through the statements of the creed, as defining the boundaries of the newly legitimate faith. To this day, someone who asks, "Are you a Christian?" is likely to follow with questions about propositional beliefs: "Do you believe that Jesus is the Son of God? Do you believe that Jesus Christ came down from heaven to save you from sin?"

The framework of canon, creed, and ecclesiastical hierarchy that Irenaeus and others began to forge in the crucible of persecution and that his successors like Athanasius worked to construct after Constantine's conversion now gained enormous appeal. The "universal" church could invite potential converts to join an assembly that not only claimed to possess certain truth and to offer eternal salvation but had also become socially acceptable, even politically advantageous. Furthermore, the structure of Christian orthodoxy has proven remarkably durable and adaptable through two millennia and is developing new forms even today throughout the world, in areas notably including Africa, North and South America, South Korea, and China.

Scholars who investigate the origins of Christianity now see, however, that the landscape we are exploring has opened up unexpected vistas. The Nag Hammadi discoveries and sources such as the Dead Sea Scrolls, along with the work of many historians today, are opening up not only Christianity as we knew it but much that lay beyond its boundaries—as we used to define them.

—

The events sketched here obviously affect the way we understand our cultural history. But for those of us who find ourselves implicated in this history, as I do, untangling some of its complex strands has practical consequences as well as intellectual ones. In my own case, the hardest—and the most exciting—thing about research into Christian beginnings has been to unlearn what I thought I knew, and to shed presuppositions I had taken for granted.

This research offers new ways to relate to religious tradition. Orthodox doctrines of God—Jewish, Christian, or Muslim—tend to emphasize the separation between what is divine and what is human: in the words of the scholar of religion Rudolph Otto, God is "wholly other" than humankind. Since those who accept such views often assume that divine revelation is diametrically opposed to human perception, they often rule out what

mystically inclined Jews and Christians have always done—
seeking to discern spiritual truth experienced as revelation, truth
that may come from intuition, reflection, or creative imagination. Christian leaders who deny that such experience can teach
us anything about God have often identified themselves as
guardians of an unchanging tradition, whose "faithfulness" consists in handing down only what they received from ancient
witnesses, neither adding nor subtracting anything. And while
church leaders believe that this view of their role expresses appropriate humility, some also understand that it invests them, as
guardians of divine truth, with God's own authority.

Such leaders could not, of course, ban the imagination
entirely—nor was this their intention. But they effectively
channeled the religious imagination of most Christians to
express—and to support—what they already taught. The two-
thousand-year legacy of Christian music, art, architecture, poetry, philosophy, and theology is, of course, enormously rich,
and our culture is inconceivable apart from Christian tradition.

But those who see Christianity as offering, in Irenaeus's words,
a "very complete system of doctrines" that contain "certain truth"
often have difficulty acknowledging—much less welcoming—
diverse viewpoints, which, nevertheless, abound. Anyone who
stands within the Roman Catholic communion, for example,
knows that it embraces members who differ on topics ranging
from doctrine to discipline, and the same applies, of course, to
virtually every other Christian denomination. But since Christians often adopt Irenaeus's view of controversy, many tend to
assume that only one side can speak the truth, while others
speak only lies—or evil. Many still insist that only their church,

whether Roman Catholic or Baptist, Lutheran or Greek Orthodox, Pentecostalist or Presbyterian, Jehovah's Witness or Christian Scientist—or only the group within their church with which
they agree—actually remains faithful to Jesus' teaching. Furthermore, since Christian tradition teaches that Jesus fully revealed
God two thousand years ago, innovators from Francis of Assisi
to Martin Luther, from George Fox and John Wesley to contemporary feminist and liberation theologians, often have disguised
innovation—sometimes even from themselves—by claiming that
they are not introducing anything new but only clarifying what
Jesus actually meant all along.

Necessary as it seemed to Irenaeus in the second century to
expel Valentinus's disciples as "heretics," doing so not only impoverished the churches that remained but also impoverished
those he expelled. Uprooted from their original home within
Christian churches, those stigmatized as "heretics" often wandered alone—despite the fact that the spiritual inquiry that
engaged them found in Judaism and Christianity not only communities of origin but also primary sources of inspiration.

What such people seek, however, is often not a different "system of doctrines" so much as insights or intimations of the
divine that validate themselves in experience—what we might
call hints and glimpses offered by the luminous *epinoia*. Some
engaged on such a path pursue it in solitude; others also participate in various forms of worship, prayer, and action. Engaging in such a process requires, of course, faith. The Greek term
for *faith* is the same one often interpreted simply as *belief*, since
faith often *includes* belief, but it involves much more: the trust
that enables us to commit ourselves to what we hope and

love.[101] We noted how Tertullian ridiculed those who saw themselves more as seekers than as believers, "Since they are willing to say—and even sincerely— . . . 'This is not so,' and 'I take this to mean something different,' and 'I do not accept that.' "[102] Despite his inference that those who make such discriminations are either foolish or arrogant, it is not only "heretics" who choose which elements of tradition to accept and practice and which to reject. The sociologist Peter Berger points out that everyone who participates in such tradition today chooses among elements of tradition; for, like Judaism and other ancient traditions, Christianity has survived for thousands of years as each generation relives, reinvents, and transforms what it received.[103]

This act of choice—which the term *heresy* originally meant—leads us back to the problem that orthodoxy was invented to solve: How can we tell truth from lies? What is genuine, and thus connects us with one another and with reality, and what is shallow, self-serving, or evil? Anyone who has seen foolishness, sentimentality, delusion, and murderous rage disguised as God's truth knows that there is no easy answer to the problem that the ancients called discernment of spirits. Orthodoxy tends to distrust our capacity to make such discriminations and insists on making them for us. Given the notorious human capacity for self-deception, we can, to an extent, thank the church for this. Many of us, wishing to be spared hard work, gladly accept what tradition teaches.

But the fact that we have no simple answer does not mean that we can evade the question. We have also seen the hazards—even terrible harm—that sometimes result from unquestioning acceptance of religious authority. Most of us, sooner or later, find that, at critical points in our lives, we must strike out on our own to make a path where none exists. What I have come to love in the wealth and diversity of our religious traditions—and the communities that sustain them—is that they offer the testimony of innumerable people to spiritual discovery. Thus they encourage those who endeavor, in Jesus' words, to "seek, and you shall find."[104]

ACKNOWLEDGMENTS

This book is based on research originally presented, for the most part, in scholarly publications (cited in each chapter's notes) and revised to make it more generally accessible. During the seven years of research and writing and revision, I have consulted with many colleagues and friends, from whom I have learned much. First, I am enormously grateful to those who generously took the time to read the manuscript and to offer corrections and criticism, and I mention in particular Glen Bowersock, Karen King, Helmut Koester, and Alexander Nehamas. And I wish to thank those whose comments and criticism helped improve portions of the work as it was in process, especially Daniel Boyarin, Ismo Dunderberg, Father Thomas Keating, Shaya Isenberg, and Stephen Mitchell, as well as April De Conick, Birger Pearson, Louis Painchaud, John Turner, and Robert McLeod Wilson, who commented on the sources presented in chapter 2; members of the Davis Seminar at Princeton University, where the research presented in chapters 3–5 was first presented, especially Anthony Grafton, who chaired the Seminar in 2001–2002, and to those who participated in it, including Peter Brown, Virginia Burrus, Susanna Elm, Rebecca Lyman, and Raymond van Dam, as well as Harry Attridge, Paula Fredriksen, Michael Stone, and Annette Reed. I owe special thanks to my colleagues John Gager, Martha Himmelfarb, and Peter Schafer, for our collegial conversations and for their willingness to check the accuracy of portions of the manuscript, and to Professor Alain Le Boulluec for his helpful comments on an earlier draft, which enabled me to make needed corrections and qualifications. None of us in the Department of Religion at Princeton could accomplish what we undertake without the kindness and invaluable support of department manager Lorraine Fuhrmann, as well as Pat Bogdziewicz and Kerry Smith. I owe many thanks, too, to Margaret Appleby, for her intelligent and resourceful research investigations, and for her expert intervention with the computer.

Research and writing for this book were completed when I was a visitor at the School of Historical Studies at the Institute for Advanced Study in Princeton, during a year of sabbatical from Princeton University in 2001–2002. I am very grateful to the faculty of that school, especially to Giles Constable and Glen Bowersock, who chaired it during the past two years, for their gracious hospitality and for making available to me, as to many others, the serene and collegial environment that the Institute offers. A grant from the Ford Foundation enabled me to take the full year of sabbatical at the Institute; for this I am especially grateful to Constance Buchanan, senior program officer, for the vision, encouragement, and support for which she is well known among our colleagues, and much loved.

There are certain people without whose participation I cannot imagine having written this book. I am very grateful to have worked with Jason Epstein, whose extraordinary gifts as an editor are well known. Over the years, our collaboration and our friendship, with its many conversations, challenges, and marvelous lunches and dinners, has become, for me, an indispensable and enjoyable part of the writing process. John Brockman and Katinka Matson, both longtime friends as well, have contributed to this project in innumerable ways. I am grateful to Ann Godoff, editor in chief and president of Random House at the time the book was written, for her leadership and enthusiastic support, and to Lynn Nesbit, for her generosity of spirit and her enormously perceptive understanding of publishing. I am very grateful to Kate Medina for graciously taking on this book as editor after that time, and contributing to its production her fine insight and generous encouragement. I wish to thank Will Murphy for his excellent suggestions, and for all he has contributed in the process of production; Meredith Blum and Jessica Kirshner, for their care in arranging many details of publication; Benjamin Dreyer, for his careful, excellent supervision of the copyediting; and Catherine Cooney, for her expertise in helping find the Coptic Fayuum portrait on the cover. I owe special thanks to the Rev. Peter Gomes for his invitation to deliver the Noble Lectures at Harvard University, and for the extraordinarily generous hospitality that he offered—along with his colleague the Rev. Dorothy Austin—as well as his helpful and critical comments, and those of other respondents, including Krister Stendahl and Paula Fredriksen, which certainly have helped improve this book.

The most personal gratitude goes to my husband, Kent Greenawalt, for his willingness to read the manuscript in process, and whose incisive understanding and generous encouragement contributed so much to the process; and to members of our family, whose presence offers so much joy: Sarah, Dave, Robert, Carla, Sasha, Claire, and Andrei.

Finally, I am very grateful to those colleagues who have allowed me to read their work in progress in manuscript form, and mention in particular Karen King's important new book, *What Is Gnosticism?*, and her new edition and commentary on *The Gospel of Mary*; Bart Ehrman's forthcoming book, *Lost Christianities*, with his incisive analysis of the sources and their implications; Marvin Meyer's new book, *Secret Gospels*; and Daniel Boyarin's book still, as of this writing, in the process of completion. Having benefited from conversations with Daniel Boyarin about his most recent manuscript, as well as from his earlier publications, I regret that I read *Border Lines: The Idea of Orthodoxy and the Partitioning of Judeo Christianity*, forthcoming in 2004 from the University of Pennsylvania Press, too late to incorporate its insights into this present work.

NOTES

CHAPTER ONE: FROM THE FEAST OF AGAPE TO THE NICENE CREED

1. I Corinthians 15:3–4.
2. So Adolf von Harnack reconstructed the origin of such statements; see *History of Dogma*, volume I, 5–6, and II, 1–2, in Neil Buchanan's translation from the 1900 edition of *Dogmengeschichte* (New York, 1961), volume I, 267–313, and II, 1–29.
3. Irenaeus, *Libros Quinque Adversus Haereses* 2.32.4, ed. W. W. Harvey (Cambridge, 1851), hereafter cited as AH.
4. Tertullian, *Apology* 39.
5. Rodney Stark, *The Rise of Christianity: A Sociologist Reconsiders History* (Princeton, 1996), especially 73–94.
6. From Galen's (lost) summary of Plato's *Republic*, preserved in Arabic and translated by R. Walzer, *Galen on Jews and Christians* (London, 1949), 15.
7. Mark 12:29–31; see also Deuteronomy 6:4.
8. Stark, *Rise of Christianity*, 86–87.
9. Matthew 25:35–49.
10. Tertullian, *Apology* 39.
11. Ibid.
12. Romans 6:3–14.
13. Tertullian, *Apology* 3.
14. Ibid., 2; for Tacitus' views, see his own words in *Annales* 15.44.2–8.
15. *Passio Sanctarum Perpetuae et Felicitatis* 3.1–2.
16. Ibid., 3.3.
17. Ibid., 5.2–4.

18. Ibid., 5:5.
19. Ibid., 6:5.
20. Ibid., 18.2.
21. Justin, I *Apology* 61.
22. Ibid., 14.
23. If, that is, we can take Justin's account as indicating common practice. Scholars often have assumed that Justin described the practices of Roman Christians—indeed, of all Roman Christians—but more recent study has modified this assumption; see, for example, George La Piana, "The Roman Church at the End of the Second Century," *Harvard Theological Review* 17 (1925), 214–277; then A. Hamman, "Valeur et signification des renseignements liturgiques de Justin," *Studia Patristica* 13 (1975), 264–274; also Paul F. Bradshaw's incisive cautionary remarks in *The Search for the Origins of Christian Worship: Sources and Methods for the Study of Early Liturgy* (Cambridge, 1992), 111–113.
24. See Bradshaw's overview of the evidence and the problems in *Search for the Origins.*
25. Here I am following the dating suggested by Jonathan Draper in, for example, his article "Torah and Troublesome Apostles in the *Didache* Community," in J. Draper, ed., *The Didache in Modern Research* (Leiden, New York, and Cologne, 1996), 340–363.
26. Didache 1.2.
27. Ibid., 1.3–5.
28. Ibid., 2.2; 4.8. The view that Didache assumes Matthew is expressed by Helmut Koester in *Synoptische Uberlieferung bei den apostolischen Väter* (Berlin, 1957), 159–241; and Bentley Layton, "The Sources, Dating, and Transmission of the Didache 1:3b–2:4," *Harvard Theological Review* 61 (1968), 343–383. Christopher Tuckett agrees that parallels with Matthew and Luke are best explained on the assumption that the Didache presupposes "the finished gospels of Matthew and Luke," 128, in "Synoptic Tradition in Di-

dache," in Draper, *Didache in Modern Research*, 92–128. I find interesting, however, the perspective Draper expresses, for example in "Christian Self-Definition Against the 'Hypocrites' in *Didache* VIII," in the same volume, 223–243, and in "The Jesus Tradition in the *Didache*," in D. Wenham, ed., *Gospel Perspectives V: The Jesus Tradition Outside the Gospels* (Sheffield, 1985), 269–289.

29. We do not know whether in this case following "the whole divine law" would have required circumcision, but certainly it did require renouncing idolatry—the worship of the gods—and probably also the practice of some version of kosher food laws. In my interpretation here, I follow Draper, "Torah and Troublesome Apostles," 352–359.

30. See also Draper, "Social Ambiguity and the Production of Text: Prophets, Teacher, Bishops, and Deacons in the Development of the Jesus Tradition in the Community of the *Didache*," in C. N. Jefford, ed., *The Didache in Context: Essays on Its Text, History, and Transmission* (Leiden, 1995), 284–313.

31. Didache 9:4. Scholars have engaged in much discussion of the Didache's account of baptism and eucharist; for a summary of views, see Bradshaw, *Search for the Origins*, 80–82, 132–136; see also Willy Rordorf, "The Didache," in *The Eucharist of the Early Christians* (New York, 1978), 1–23; John W. Riggs, "From Gracious Table to Sacramental Elements: The Tradition History of *Didache* 9 and 10," *Second Century* 4 (1984), 83–101; and Johannes Betz, "The Eucharist in the *Didache*," in Draper, *Didache in Modern Research*, 233–275.

32. Didache 10.6; see also Enrico Mazza, "Elements of a Eucharistic Interpretation," in Draper, *Didache in Modern Research*, 276–299.

33. Mark 14:22–24; compare Matthew 26:26–29; Luke 22:7–13; I Corinthians 11:23–25.

34. Tertullian, *Apology* 7.

35. Ibid., 8.

36. One contemporary anthropologist has suggested that Paul and his followers adopted this ritual to repel traditionally minded Jews and so to set themselves apart from Jewish communities.

37. Justin, I *Apology* 66. Closer parallels occur within some of the Dead Sea Scrolls; see, for example, Otto Betz, "Early Christian Cult in the Light of Qumran," *Religious Studies Bulletin* 2:2 (April 1982), 73–85.

38. Justin, I *Apology* 54. Many scholars have considered the parallels between the rituals practiced in mystery religions and the Christian eucharist; see, for example, E. Lohse, *The New Testament Environment* (London, 1976), and more recently, A.J.M. Wedderburn, "The Soteriology of the Mysteries and Pauline Baptismal Theology," *Novum Testamentum* 19:1 (1982) 53–72, and "Hellenistic Christian Traditions in Romans 6?" in *New Testament Studies* 29 (1983), 337–355.

39. I Corinthians 1:23. The Greek term is *skandalon*.

40. For the latter phrase, I am indebted to N. T. Wright, *Jesus and the Victory of God* (Minneapolis, 1992).

41. Luke 24:21.

42. Mark 8:31. Mark uses the Greek term *dei*, usually translated "it is necessary."

43. Mark 14:22. See note 50 on references to studies of the "words of institution."

44. Mark 14:24. On the sacrificial imagery, see Edward J. Kilmartin, S.J., "Sacrificium Laudis: Content and Function of Early Eucharistic Prayers," *Theological Studies* 35:2 (June 1974), 268–286.

45. Matthew 26:27–28.

46. Exodus 24:8.

47. On Mark's allusions to the Mosaic covenant, see the summary in Reginald Fuller, "The Double Origin of the Eucharist," in *Biblical Research: Papers of the Chicago Society of Biblical Research VIII* (Chicago, 1963), 60–72; see also Joachim Jeremias, *Die Abendsmahlworte Jesu*

(Göttingen, 1949), translated as *The Eucharistic Words of Jesus* (London and New York, 1966).

48. Jeremiah 31:31–34.

49. On Paul's interpretation of the words, see, for example, Eduard Schweitzer, *The Lord's Supper According to the New Testament* (Philadelphia, 1967); also Paul Neuenzeit, *Das Herrenmahl: Studien zur paulinischen Eucharistieauffassung* (Munich, 1960).

50. For a summary of discussion and for references, see Bradshaw, *Search for the Origins*, 48–51. On sacrifice, see, for example, Robert Daly, *The Origins of the Christian Doctrine of Sacrifice* (London and New York, 1986); and Rowan Williams, *Eucharistic Sacrifice: The Roots of a Metaphor* (Bramcote, Notts, 1982).

51. Justin, I *Apology* 67. But see, for example, the references in note 23, which question whether—or to what extent—Justin describes actual practices, and if so, which he may have in mind.

52. I Corinthians 5:7.

53. Mark 14:12–16.

54. Luke 22:15.

55. Luke 22:19b; I Corinthians 11:24–25.

56. John 13:1.

57. John 19:14.

58. For discussion of John's view of the passion narrative in general, and his special chronology in particular, see Raymond E. Brown, S.J., *The Death of the Messiah: From Gethsemane to the Grave* (New York, London, Toronto, Sydney, and Auckland, 1993).

59. John 19:34.

60. Although John does not offer an account of the "Last Supper," in the John account Jesus does urge his disciples to eat "[his] flesh" and to drink "[his] blood" (6:35–58).

61. Exodus 12:46. The Revised Standard Version offers here a translation that makes the passage sound as if it applied to Jesus, not to a sacrificial animal: "Not a bone of *him* shall be broken."

62. John 19:36.

63. John 6:35–60.

64. I Corinthians 11:26.

65. Apocalypse of Peter 81:10–11. The sign that Constantine later adopted, although often seen as a cross, actually consisted instead of the first two letters of the title *Christ.*

66. See Chapter 4 for discussion and references.

67. Gershom Scholem, the great scholar of Jewish texts, wrote that "myth is the story line to a ritual" (*On the Kabbalah and Its Symbolism* [New York, 1969], 132–133); and while some might object to applying the term *myth* to the gospels, since they relate events attested actually to have happened, the story of Jesus, as the gospels tell it is, if not a myth, a story intended to convey meaning.

68. Professor Helmut Koester, my first and invaluable mentor in the history of Christianity, has demonstrated in a wide range of articles how the early accounts of the gospel are connected with liturgical celebration. See, for example, his recent article "The Memory of Jesus' Death and the Worship of the Risen Lord," *Harvard Theological Review* 91:1 (1998), 335–350.

69. The Greek term *koinonia* can be translated "communion" or "participation," in passages such as I Corinthians 10:16: "The cup of blessing which we bless, is it not a *koinonia* in the blood of Christ: The bread which we break, is it not a *koinonia* in the body of Christ?"

70. I Corinthians 10:17; Galatians 3:28; I Corinthians 10:3–4.

71. Justin, I *Apology* 61; see also 65–66.

72. For discussion, see my earlier book *The Gnostic Gospels* (New York, 1979); and I especially recommend to the interested reader several important recent discussions that, to my regret, were not available to me during the time I was writing: Bart Ehrman, *Lost Christianities* (New York, 2003); Marvin Meyer, *Secret Gospels* (San Francisco, 2003); and Richard Valantasis, *The Gospel of Thomas* (London, New York, 1997).

73. The work of many scholars today is changing our earlier, more simplistic picture of the origins of Christianity. Among notable books being published currently see, for example, Daniel Boyarin, *Border Lines: The Idea of Orthodoxy and the Partitioning of Judeo-Christianity* (Pennsylvania, 2004); Bart Ehrman, *Lost Christianities* (New York and London, 2003); Karen King, *What Is Gnosticism?* (Cambridge, 2003); Marvin Myer, *Secret Gospels* (California, 2003). I am enormously grateful to these colleagues for allowing me to read each of these books in manuscript.

CHAPTER TWO: GOSPELS IN CONFLICT

This chapter condenses and summarizes research that is presented in a fuller and more technical form as Elaine Pagels, "Exegesis of Genesis 1 in the Gospels of Thomas and John," *Journal of Biblical Literature* 118 (1999), 477–496.

1. John 15:12, 17.
2. John 3:18.
3. John 8:44. For discussion and references on how John's gospel, as well as the others, portrays "the Jews," see Elaine Pagels, *The Origin of Satan* (New York, 1995), especially 89–111, and the references cited there.
4. For the authoritative account of the story of the discovery, see James M. Robinson, "The Discovery of the Nag Hammadi Codices," *Biblical Archaeologist* 42 (1979), 206–224.
5. Irenaeus, AH 1, *Praefatio*.
6. Gospel of Thomas 70, in Nag Hammadi Library (hereafter NHL) 126, where this difficult passage is translated differently and, in my view, less lucidly. Throughout the present text, I have taken liberties with NHL translations in the interest of clarity or of preserving the poetic quality of the original text; thus, readers who consult the NHL may note variations.
7. See the incisive book by Michael Williams, *Rethinking Gnosticism:*

An Argument for Dismantling a Dubious Category (Princeton, 1996); and most recently, Karen King's major new book, *What Is Gnosticism?* (Cambridge, 2003). See also Bentley Layton, "Prolegomena to the Study of Ancient Gnosticism," in I. M. White and O. L. Yarbrough, eds., *The Social World of the Early Christians: Essays in Honor of Wayne A. Meeks* (Minneapolis, 1995), 334–350; as well as the thoughtful essay by Antti Marjanen, "Is Thomas a Gnostic Gospel?" in the outstanding collection edited by Risto Uro, *Thomas at the Crossroads: Essays on the Gospel of Thomas* (Edinburgh, 1998), 107–139. James Robinson also edited a one-volume English translation of all the texts discovered as *The Nag Hammadi Library in English* (San Francisco, 1977); Bentley Layton later published another translation as *The Gnostic Scriptures* (New York, 1987). The most complete edition available in English, however, is *The Nag Hammadi Series*, over twenty volumes published by Brill Press in the Netherlands, which include the Coptic texts with English introductions, translations, and notes.

8. See, for example, Steven Davies, *The Gospel of Thomas and Wisdom Tradition* (New York, 1963); Stephen J. Patterson, *The Gospel of Thomas and Jesus* (Sonoma, Calif., 1993); Gregory J. Riley, *Resurrection Reconsidered: Thomas and John in Controversy* (Minneapolis, 1995); April De Conick, *Seek to See Him: Ascent and Vision Mysticism in the "Gospel of Thomas"* (Leiden, New York, and Cologne, 1996); also her fascinating essay "'Blessed are those who have not seen' (John 20:29): Johannine Dramatization of an Early Christian Discourse," in J. D. Turner and A. McGuire, eds., *The Nag Hammadi Library After Fifty Years* (Leiden, New York, and Cologne, 1997), 381–400.

9. John 20:8; yet see the incisive critique of this kind of usage in Paul-Hubert Poirier, "The Writings Ascribed to Thomas and the Thomas Tradition," in Turner and McGuire, *Nag Hammadi Library After Fifty Years*, 295–397.

10. For discussion, see Chapter 4; also, among the many scholarly

works on this issue, Maurice F. Wiles, *The Spiritual Gospel: The Interpretation of the Fourth Gospel in the Early Church* (Cambridge, 1960); T. E. Pollard, *Johannine Christology and the Early Church* (Cambridge, 1970); C. H. Dodd, *Interpretation of the Fourth Gospel* (Cambridge, 1953); and E. Pagels, *The Johannine Gospel in Gnostic Exegesis* (Nashville, 1973).

11. Mark 11:15–16.

12. Mark 11:18.

13. John 2:15.

14. John 12:10.

15. John 11:48.

16. Origen, *Commentary on John* 10.4–6.

17. John 10:33.

18. John 20:28.

19. Origen, *Commentary on John* 1.6.

20. For discussion of the titles "son of God" and "messiah," see the influential work of Bart Ehrman, *The New Testament: A Historical Introduction to the Early Christian Writings* (Oxford and New York, 2000), 60–84. For an excellent discussion of various Christologies, see Pheme Perkins, "New Testament Christologies in Gnostic Transformation," in *The Future of Early Christianity: Essays in Honor of Helmut Koester* Birger A. Pearson, ed., (Minneapolis, 1991), 422–441.

21. John 20:28.

22. For a masterful discussion of the traditions preserved in Thomas and their relation to the synoptic gospels and to John, see Helmut Koester, *Ancient Christian Gospels: Their History and Development* (London and Philadelphia, 1990), especially 75–127.

23. For an overview of discussion of Thomas tradition, see Poirier, "The Writings Ascribed to Thomas."

24. Koester, *Ancient Christian Gospels*, 78–80; see also the incisive assessment of Philip Sellew, "The Gospel of Thomas: Prospects for Future Research," in Turner and McGuire, *Nag Hammadi Library*

After Fifty Years, 327–346; also Jean-Marie Sevrin, "L'Interprétation de l' évangile selon Thomas, entre tradition et rédaction," in the same volume, 347–360.

25. Gospel of Thomas 1, in NHL 118.
26. Genesis 1:3. For an excellent discussion, see Steven Davies, "Christology and Protology in the Gospel of John," *Journal of Biblical Literature* 111 (1992), 663–683.
27. John 1:3.
28. Koester, *Ancient Christian Gospels,* 86–128; see also Patterson, *Gospel of Thomas and Jesus.*
29. John 1:9; the Greek phrase *phos ton anthropon* can be translated "light of human beings."
30. Genesis 1:26–27; again, for a more detailed and technical version of the discussion presented in this chapter, see Pagels, "Exegesis of Genesis 1."
31. A term that may have been coined by Irenaeus: AH 3.11.8.
32. Ibid., 1.20.1.
33. Mark 8:27–29.
34. Mark 15:39.
35. Psalm 2:7; for discussion of the way such passages are worked into the birth stories of Matthew and Luke, see Raymond E. Brown, S.J., *The Birth of the Messiah: A Commentary on the Infancy Narratives in Matthew and Luke,* 2nd ed. (New York, 1993).
36. Mark 1:1.
37. See, for example, Ezekiel 2:1; 2:8; 3:1; 3:4; 3:10; 3:17; 3:25; and throughout the oracles of Ezekiel.
38. Daniel 7:13.
39. Mark 14:61–62.
40. Most scholars agree that the author of Luke also wrote the New Testament Acts of the Apostles; see Acts 2:22–23, 32–36.
41. John 1.1.
42. Philippians 2:7–8.
43. I Corinthians 12:3.

44. Ignatius, *Letter to the Romans* 6:3.

45. Pliny, *Letter* 10.96.7; see discussion of the pre-Pauline "Christ hymn" of Philippians 2 in Ralph P. Martin's fine monograph *Carmen Christi* (London, 1967).

46. On composition, see Koester, *Ancient Christian Gospels*, 80 ff.; and more recently, the incisive comments of Risto Uro, in his introduction to *Thomas at the Crossroads*, 1–32.

47. Matthew, for example, includes the famous saying that "many are called, but few are chosen" (22:14); Thomas has Jesus say, "I shall choose you, one out of a thousand, and two out of ten thousand" (saying 23, in NHL 121). John's version, too, has Jesus emphasize divine initiative in the process: "You did not choose me, but I chose you" (15:16; see also 13:18).

48. Matthew 16:17.

49. Gospel of Thomas 13, in NHL 119.

50. Ibid., 50, in NHL 123.

51. Mark 1:1–4.

52. Mark 1:15.

53. Mark 9:1.

54. Mark 13:2.

55. Mark 13:8–19.

56. Mark 13:24–26.

57. Mark 13:30–33.

58. John 5:25.

59. John 11:24.

60. Gospel of Thomas 3, in NHL 118.

61. Mark 13:2–37.

62. Gospel of Thomas 51, in NHL 123.

63. Ibid., 113, in NHL 130.

64. Luke 17:20–21.

65. Thomas Merton, quoted by Marcus Borg, in *Meeting Jesus Again for the First Time: The Historical Jesus and the Heart of Contemporary Faith* (San Francisco, 1994).

66. Gospel of Mary 8:15–20. See the major new edition and commentary by Karen King, forthcoming (as of this writing) from Harvard University Press.

67. Luke 21:34–36.

68. John 1:1.

69. Genesis 1:2.

70. Genesis 1:3.

71. John 1:9.

72. Gospel of Thomas 16, in NHL 120.

73. Ibid., 77, in NHL 126.

74. Ibid., 2, in NHL 118.

75. Ibid., 3, in NHL 118.

76. Ibid., 70, translation by Professor George MacRae, offered in class. As stated in note 6, the NHL translation of this difficult saying differs, and I find it less lucid.

77. Ibid., 6, in NHL 118.

78. Matthew 6:3–4.

79. Matthew 6:17.

80. Matthew 7:9–13.

81. Gospel of Thomas 6, in NHL 118.

82. Ibid., 91, in NHL 128.

83. Plotinus, *Ennead* 5, *Against the Gnostics.*

84. Gospel of Thomas 3, in NHL 118.

85. Ibid., 19, in NHL 120.

86. See, for example, On the Origin of the World 108.7–9, in NHL 177; Eugnostos 76.14–81.12, in NHL 228–232; Apocryphon (Secret Book) of John II, 14.13–15.13, in NHL 113; for a more complete edition, comparing the available manuscripts, see Frederick Wisse and Michael Waldstein, eds., *The Apocryphon of John: A Synopsis of Nag Hammadi Codices II, 1; III, 1; and IV, 1 with BG 8502, 2* (Nag Hammadi and Manichaean Studies 33, Leiden, 1995), 82–89.

87. Irenaeus, AH 1.30.1. For references, see Pagels, "Exegesis of Genesis 1," 202–205; and for a masterful discussion, see Hans–Martin

Schenke, *Der Gott "Mensch" in der Gnosis: Ein religionsgeschichtlicher Beitrag zur Diskussion über die paulinische Anschauung von der Kirche als Leib Christi* (Göttingen, 1962); and the fascinating articles by Gilles Quispel, "Der Gnostiche *Anthropos* und die jüdische Tradition," *Eranos Jahrbuch* 22 (1953), 195–234, and "Ezekiel 1:26 in Jewish Mysticism and Gnosis," *Vigiliae Christianae* 34 (1980), 1–13.

88. For a classic discussion see Gershom Scholem, *Major Trends in Jewish Mysticism* (New York, 1965); see also Ithamar Gruenwald, *Apocalyptic and Merkavah Mysticism* (Leiden, 1980), and *From Apocalypticism to Gnosticism: Studies in Apocalypticism, Merkavah Mysticism and Gnosticism* (Frankfurt, Bern, New York, and Paris, 1988); Moshe Idel, *Kabbalah: New Perspectives* (New Haven, 1988); Elliot Wolfson, *Through a Speculum That Shines: Vision and Imagination in Medieval Jewish Mysticism* (Princeton, 1994); and Peter Schäfer, *The Hidden and Manifest God: Some Major Themes in Early Jewish Mysticism* (Albany, 1992).

89. Gospel of Thomas 50, in NHL 123.

90. Ibid., 24, in NHL 121.

91. Ibid., 84, in NHL 127.

92. I am grateful to Stephen Mitchell for his insight and his translation; for this poem, see *Meetings with the Archangel* (New York, 1998), 137.

93. Gospel of Thomas 2, in NHL 118.

94. Ibid., 108, in NHL 129.

95. Book of Thomas the Contender 138.7–19, in NHL 189.

96. John 11:16; for discussion, see Riley, *Resurrection Reconsidered.*

97. For a discussion of the composition of this gospel, see, for example, Raymond E. Brown, S.J., *The Gospel According to John: Introduction, Translation, and Notes* (Garden City, N.Y., 1966).

98. John 21:20–24. Most scholars regard this chapter as an addition to the original text; see, for example, Brown's discussion of chapter 21 in *Gospel According to John.*

99. Matthew 1:18.

100. Matthew 16:17.

101. This disciple appears, for example, in John 13:23.

102. John 13:24–25.

103. John 19:35.

104. John 20:3–8.

105. John 21:7.

106. John 21:17.

107. For discussion, see the forthcoming edition of the Gospel of Mary by Karen King; see also the excellent article by Risto Uro, " 'Who will be our leader?' Authority and Autonomy in the Gospel of Thomas," in *Fair Play: Diversity and Conflicts in Early Christianity: Essays in Honour of Heikki Räisänen* (Leiden and Boston, 2002), 457–485. See also the very interesting work of Richard Valantasis, *Spiritual Guides of the Third Century: A Semiotic Study of the Guide-Disciple Relationship in Christianity, Neoplatonism, Hermetism, and Gnosticism* (Minneapolis, 1991).

108. John 20:30–31.

109. John 20:28.

110. Louis Martyn's groundbreaking work, *History and Theology in the Fourth Gospel* (Nashville, 1979), suggests that the story told in John 9 is, in effect, that of John's community. Martyn's influential thesis has been modified by the critique of other scholars who question especially his assumptions about the formation and use of the so-called *birkat ha mininm*; see Asher Finkel, "Yavneh's Liturgy and Early Christianity," *Journal of Ecumenical Studies* 18:2 (1981), 231–250; William Horbury, "The Benediction of the Minim and Early Jewish–Christian Controversy," *Journal of Theological Studies* 33 (1982); Alan F. Segal, "Ruler of This World: Attitudes About Mediator Figures and the Importance of Sociology for Self-Definition," in E. P. Sanders, ed., *Jewish and Christian Self-Definition*, volume II (Philadelphia, 1980), 245–268; and the very intriguing recently published article by Daniel Boyarin, "The

Gospel of the Memra: Jewish Binitarianism and the Prologue to John," *Harvard Theological Review* 94:3 (2001), 243 ff.

111. John 1:1–41.
112. John 9:7.
113. John 9:22.
114. John 9:38.
115. John 9:39.
116. John 10:8–9.
117. John 8:58.
118. Exodus 3:14.
119. John 19:2.
120. John 3:18.
121. Galatians 3:4.
122. John 1:1–4.
123. John 1:5.
124. John 1:10.
125. John 1:11.
126. John 1:14.
127. Ibid.
128. 1 John 1:1.
129. I am grateful to my colleague Alexander Nehamas for pointing out that this Greek term strongly connotes singularity, a usage that goes back as far as Parmenides' description of what he called being (*tō ōn*).
130. John 14:1.
131. John 15:12.
132. John 15:12–24.
133. Gospel of Thomas 22, in NHL 121.
134. John 8:12.
135. John 8:23.
136. John 8:24.
137. John 1:29.

138. John 3:5.

139. John 6:53–55.

140. In his remarkable monograph *Resurrection Reconsidered.*

141. John 11:16; see Riley's discussion in *Resurrection Reconsidered,* 100–180.

142. John 14:3–4.

143. John 14:6.

144. Luke 24:33–36.

145. Matthew 28:10.

146. John 20:24.

147. John 20:19–23.

148. John 20:28.

149. John 20:29.

150. John 21:24–25.

151. Irenaeus, AH 3.11.1–3.

152. C. H. Dodd, in his commentary on the Johannine gospel, notes that this is what separates John's message from "gnostics"; for Dodd, this secures John's place as an authentically Christian teacher; see *Interpretation of the Fourth Gospel,* 97–114, 250–285.

CHAPTER THREE: GOD'S WORD OR HUMAN WORDS?

For the technical discussion of the research summarized in this chapter, see Elaine Pagels, "Irenaeus, the 'Canon of Truth' and the Gospel of John: 'Making a Difference' Through Hermeneutics and Ritual," *Vigiliae Christianae* 56.4 (2002), 339–371.

1. Theodor Gaster's comment occurred in a conversation; Buber's phrase serves as the title of his book *I and Thou* (translated by W. Kaufmann from *Ich und du* and published in New York, 1970).

2. Raymond E. Brown, S.J.; this paraphrases the end of his review of *The Gnostic Gospels, New York Times,* November 1979.

3. Tertullian, *Apology* 1.

4. Ibid., 2.

5. *Martyrdom of St. Polycarp* 3 f.

6. Pliny, *Letter* 10.96.3.

7. *Martyrdom of St. Justin and His Companions,* Recension A, 3.2. The place name has been corrupted in the manuscripts; I follow the reading of Herbert Musurillo, *The Acts of the Christian Martyrs* (Oxford, 1972), 45.

8. Origen, *Contra Celsum* 3.54.

9. Tertullian, *Apology* 50.

10. *Martyrdom of St. Polycarp* 12.

11. So, at least, the author of his Martyrdom represents him; see chapter 8.

12. Irenaeus, AH 3.3.4.

13. Ibid.

14. Polycarp, *Letter to the Philippians* 6.3.

15. Irenaeus, AH 3.3.4.

16. For discussion and references concerning Tatian's *Diatessaron,* see Koester, *Ancient Christian Gospels,* 403–430.

17. Irenaeus, AH 3.11.8.

18. Markus Bockmuehl, " 'To Be or Not to Be': The Possible Futures of New Testament Scholarship," *Scottish Journal of Theology* 51:3 (1998), 271–306.

19. *Martyrdom of St. Polycarp* 6–15.

20. W.H.C. Frend, *Martyrdom and Persecution in the Early Church* (Oxford, 1965; New York, 1967), 5–6.

21. *The Letters of the Churches of Lyons and Vienne,* I.10.

22. Eusebius, *Historia Ecclesiae,* quoting Apollinarius, in 5.16.5.

23. Ibid., 5.17.12; for a careful account of the controversy, see Christine Trevett, *Montanism: Gender, Authority, and the New Prophecy* (Cambridge, 1996); among ancient authors, a primary source is Eusebius's account in 5.16.1–19.2. For an edition of the sayings attributed to the prophets, see Kurt Aland, "Der Montanismus und die Kleinasiatische Theologie," *Zeitschrift für Neue Testamenten Wissenschaft* 46 (1955), 109–116.

24. Eusebius, *Historia Ecclesiae* 5.16.17; Aland, *Montanismus,* saying 16.

25. John 16:4. See the intriguing and provocative article by M. E. Boring, "The Influence of Christian Prophecy on the Johannine Portrayal of the Paraclete and Jesus," *New Testament Studies* 25 (1978), 113–122; see also *Sayings of the Risen Christ: Christian Prophecy in the Synoptic Tradition* (Cambridge, 1982); R. E. Heine, "The Role of the Gospel of John in the Montanist Controversy," *Second Century* 6 (1987), 1–18; see also his article "The Gospel of John and the Montanist Debate at Rome," *Studia Patristica* 21 (1989), 95–100; and Dennis E. Groh, "Utterance and Exegesis: Biblical Interpretation in the Montanist Crisis," in D. E. Groh and R. Jewett, eds., *The Living Text* (New York, 1985), 73–95.

26. Irenaeus, AH 3.11.9; Eusebius, *Historia Ecclesiae* 3.28.1; see Dionysios bar Salibi, *Commentary on the Apocalypse* 1.

27. *On Modesty,* 21. On Tertullian, see Timothy D. Barnes, *Tertullian: A Historical and Literary Study* (Oxford, 1971).

28. On the media of revelation, see David E. Aune, *Prophecy in Early Christianity and the Ancient Mediterranean World* (Grand Rapids, 1983); on Valentinus, see the definitive study by Christoph Markschies, *Valentinus Gnosticus? Untersuchungen zur valentinianischen Gnosis mit einem Kommentar zu den Fragmenten Valentins* (Tübingen, 1992).

29. Eusebius, *Historia Ecclesiae* 5.20.4.

30. Mark 1:10–11.

31. Luke 2:8–13.

32. Luke 24:34.

33. Acts 2:17–21; Joel 2:28–32.

34. I Corinthians 1:1; 15:3–11.

35. II Corinthians 12:4.

36. John 16:13.

37. Revelation 1:10–19.

38. Acts 2:1–4.

39. *Martyrdom of Saints Perpetua and Felicitas* 1.

40. So indicates the Muratorian Fragment, a source taken by Harnack and others to be from the late second century but recently dated more persuasively by A. C. Sundberg to the fourth century; see "Towards a Revised History of the New Testament Canon," *Studia Evangelica* 4 (1968), 452–461; and see the fuller study by Geoffrey M. Hahneman, *The Muratorian Fragment and the Development of the Canon* (Oxford Theological Monographs, Oxford, 1992).

41. Acts 1:9–11.

42. *Martyrdom of St. Polycarp* 5.

43. Irenaeus, AH 5.6.1.

44. Ibid., 2.32.4.

45. Ibid.

46. Ibid., 3.11.9.

47. Ibid., 2.13.8.

48. Ibid., 1.13.1. This discussion paraphrases, to some extent, what is described in Pagels, *Gnostic Gospels*, 59–61.

49. Ibid. Marcus's prayer alludes to Matthew 18:10.

50. Irenaeus, AH 1.13.3.

51. Ibid., 1.13.4; see Acts 1:17–26.

52. Irenaeus, AH 1.14.1.

53. Ibid., 1.14.4.

54. See, for more recent discussion, Moshe Idel, *Kabbalah: New Perspectives* (New Haven, 1988). Idel, following previous scholars, including Moses Gaster, sees Marcus's teaching drawing upon Jewish theological speculations and practice. For a major recent contribution, see Niclas Förster's important monograph, *Marcus Magus: Kult, Lehre, und Gemeindeleben einer valentinianischen Gnostikergruppe: Sammlung der Quellen und Kommentar* (Tübingen, 1999).

55. Cf. Genesis 1:3.

56. Irenaeus, AH 1.14.8.

57. Ibid., 1.14.1.

58. Here Irenaeus's polemic echoes that of an admired predecessor whom he calls "the holy elder" (*presbyter:* the term is sometimes translated "priest," but this may be a later connotation); ibid., 1.15.6.

59. Ibid., 1.18.1.

60. Ibid., 1.20.1.

61. For discussion of the Secret Book of John and the Gospel of Truth and how such writings interpret "the Scriptures," see Chapter 4; for some recent articles on gnostic exegesis, see, for example, Pheme Perkins, "Spirit and Letter: Poking Holes in the Canon," *Journal of Religion* (1996), 307–327; Harold W. Attridge, "The Gospel of Truth as an Exoteric Text," in *Nag Hammadi, Gnosticism, and Early Christianity* C. W. Hedrick and R. Hodgson, eds., (Peabody, Mass., 1986), 239–255; Patricia Cox Miller, " 'Words with an Alien Voice': Gnostics, Scripture, and Canon," *Journal of the American Academy of Religion* 57 (1989), 459–483; Robert M. Grant, *Heresy and Criticism: The Search for Authenticity in Early Christian Literature* (Louisville, Ky., 1993); and Louis Painchaud, "The Use of Scripture in Gnostic Literature," *Journal of Early Christian Studies* 4:2 (1996), 129–146.

62. For discussion, see Chapter 5; of the many scholarly discussions, see, among recent articles, David Brakke, "Canon Formation and Social Conflict in Fourth Century Egypt," *Harvard Theological Review* 87:4 (1994), 395–419, as well as his illuminating book *Athanasius and the Politics of Asceticism* (Baltimore and London, 1995).

63. Acts 1:9.

64. Apocryphon of James 2:9–15, in NHL 30.

65. Ibid., 2:19–25, in NHL 30.

66. Ibid., 3:35–4:27, especially 4:19, in NHL 31.

67. Ibid., 5:19–20.

68. Ibid., 15:6–28. In her recent book, April De Conick evaluates this as a vision that both resembles and qualifies those she says were sought in certain circles of Jewish visionaries. See *Seek to See Him.*

69. II Corinthians 12:1–4. April De Conick and Jarl Fossum, "Stripped Before God: A New Interpretation of Logion 37 of the Gospel of Thomas," *Vigiliae Christianae* 45 (1991), 123–150; see also Alan F. Segal, "Heavenly Ascent in Hellenistic Judaism, Early Christianity, and Their Environment," *Aufstieg und Niedergang der Romischen Welt* 2:23:2 (1980), 1333–94; *Paul the Convert: The Apostolate and Apostasy of Saul the Pharisee* (New Haven and London, 1990); and C.R.A. Morray-Jones, "Paradise Revisited (2 Cor. 12:1–12): The Jewish Mystical Background of Paul's Apostolate, Part 2: Paul's Heavenly Ascent and Its Significance," *Harvard Theological Review* 86:3 (1993), 265–292. For a major critical perspective, see Martha Himmelfarb, *Ascent to Heaven in Jewish and Christian Apocalypses* (New York, 1993); "The Practice of Ascent in the Ancient Mediterranean World," in John J. Collins and M. Fishbane, eds., *Death, Ecstasy, and Other Worldly Journeys* (Albany, 1995); "Revelation and Rapture: The Transformation of the Visionary in the Ascent Apocalypses," in John J. Collins and James H. Charlesworth, eds., *Mysteries and Revelation: Apocalyptic Studies Since the Uppsala Colloquium*, JSP Supplements 9 (Sheffield, 1991); and Peter Schäfer, ed., *Synopse zur Hekhalot-Literatur* (Texte und Studien zum Antiken Judentum 2, Tübingen, 1981); *Mystik und Theologie des rabbinischen Judentums* (ed., with M. Schlüter, New York, 1992); and especially *The Hidden and Manifest God: Some Major Themes in Early Jewish Mysticism* (Albany, 1992).
70. Prayer of the Apostle Paul 1:6–9, in NHL 27.
71. Ibid., 1:26–34, in NHL 28; cf. I Corinthians 2:9–10.
72. Carol Newsom, *Songs of the Sabbath Sacrifice: A Critical Edition* (Atlanta, 1985).
73. See note 69 for references.
74. 2 Corinthians 12:3.
75. See references in note 69.
76. Isaiah 6:1–5.
77. This, at any rate, is what many took Genesis 5:24 to mean.

78. See, for example, the Books of Enoch.
79. David J. Halperin, *The Faces of the Chariot: Early Jewish Responses to Ezekiel's Vision* (Tübingen, 1988); Wolfson, *Through a Speculum That Shines.*
80. Apocalypse of Peter 71:15–25, in NHL 341.
81. Ibid., 81.10–82.15, in NHL 344.
82. Gospel of Mary 8.14–20, in NHL 472. For a new translation and discussion, see the forthcoming edition of the Gospel of Mary by Karen King.
83. Gospel of Mary, 10.1–6, in NHL 472.
84. Ibid., 10.10–25, in NHL 472.
85. Ibid., 17.7–15, in NHL 473.
86. Ibid., 17.19–18.19, in NHL 473.
87. Jeremiah 23:25–32.
88. Zechariah 9:9.
89. Matthew 21:6–7.
90. Justin, *Dialogue with Trypho* 7.
91. Ibid., 8.
92. Ibid., 9.
93. Isaiah 7:14.
94. Justin, *Dialogue with Trypho* 43.
95. Irenaeus, AH 1.11.9.
96. Ibid., 1.10.1.
97. Ibid., 1.11.8.

CHAPTER FOUR: THE CANON OF TRUTH AND THE TRIUMPH OF JOHN

For fuller and more technical discussions of the research summarized in this chapter, see Elaine Pagels, "Irenaeus, the 'Canon of Truth' and the Gospel of John: 'Making a Difference' Through Hermeneutics and Ritual," in *Vigiliae Christianae* 56.4 (2002), 339–371; also Pagels, "Ritual in the Gospel of Philip," in Turner and McGuire, *Nag Hammadi Library After Fifty Years*, 280–294; "The Mystery of

Marriage in the Gospel of Philip," in Pearson, *Future of Early Christianity*, 442–452; and *Johannine Gospel in Gnostic Exegesis*.

1. T. S. Eliot, "Ash Wednesday."

2. Irenaeus, AH 1, *Praefatio*.

3. For these fragments, with translation, along with a careful and important recent study, see Christoph Markschies, *Valentinus Gnosticus? Untersuchungen zur valentinianischen Gnosis mit einem Kommentar zu den Fragmenten Valentins* (Tübingen, 1992).

4. The title of this poem, *Theros*, can be translated "harvest" or "summer fruit." The translation I present here is my own; for other translations and for the Greek text, see Christoph Markschies, *Valentinus Gnosticus?* 218–259; see also the incisive response by Andrew McGowan, "Valentinus Poeta: Notes on *Theros*," *Vigiliae Christianae* 51.2 (1997), 158–178.

5. For discussion, see Hans von Campenhausen, *The Formation of the Christian Bible*, trans. J. A. Baker, from *Die Entstehung der christlichen Bibel*, first edited in Tübingen, 1968 (Philadelphia and London, 1972), 80–87.

6. *Letter to Flora* 3.8.

7. Irenaeus, AH 3.11.7.

8. For sources and discussion, see Pagels, *Johannine Gospel in Gnostic Exegesis*.

9. See, for example, Irenaeus, AH 1.9.4; and the discussion by R. L. Wilken, "The Homeric Cento in Irenaeus' *Adversus Haereses* 1.9.4," *Vigiliae Christianae* 21 (1967), 25–33; A. Rousseau and L. Dautreleau, *Irénée de Lyon contre les Héresies* (Paris, 1965).

10. For an excellent study of such teachings and interpretation, see the recent work of R. M. Grant, *Heresy and Criticism*. See also Robert Lamberton, *Homer the Theologian: Neoplatonist Allegorical Reading and the Growth of the Epic Tradition* (Berkeley, 1986).

11. Irenaeus, AH 2.10.1–4. For a fascinating discussion of parallels between gnostic and patristic exegesis of John's prologue, see Anne Pasquier, "Interpretation of the Prologue of John's Gos-

pel in Some Gnostic and Patristic Writings: A Common Tradition," in Turner and McGuire, *Nag Hammadi Library After Fifty Years*, 484–498.

12. See Perkins, "Spirit and Letter," 307–327.

13. John 2:13 f.

14. Origen, *Commentary on John* 10.4–6; for fuller discussion and references, see Wiles, *Spiritual Gospel*, 96 f., and Pagels, *Johannine Gospel in Gnostic Exegesis*, 66–113.

15. Valentinus 2, in Clement of Alexandria, *Stromateis* 2.14.3–6 (for discussion, see Markschies, *Valentinus Gnosticus?* 54 ff).

16. Valentinus 7, in Hippolytus, *Refutation of All Heresies* 6.42.2.

17. Gospel of Truth 29.9–25, in NHL 43.

18. Opening lines of "Dover Beach."

19. Gospel of Truth 29.9–25, in NHL 43.

20. Ibid., 30.16–21, in NHL 43.

21. Ibid., 24:5–9, in NHL 41.

22. Matthew 18:2–4; Luke 15:3–7.

23. I Corinthians 2:7.

24. Gospel of Truth 18:24–29, in NHL 38.

25. Ibid., 18.29–34, in NHL 38.

26. Ibid., 16.31–33, in NHL 37.

27. Ibid., 42.1–10, in NHL 48.

28. Ibid., 33.35–34.35, in NHL 44.

29. Ibid., 32.35–33.30,

30. I Corinthians 11:23.

31. John 13:4–5.

32. John 13:7–8.

33. "Round Dance of the Cross," in Acts of John 94.1–4. For a recently edited Greek text with French translation and notes, see E. Junod and J. P. Kästli, *Acta Johannis: Praefatio-Textus*, in *Corpus Christianorum* (Turnhout, 1983). Here I am following the recent English translation published by Barbara E. Bowe in her article "Dancing into

the Divine: The Hymn of the Dance in the *Acts of John*," *Journal of Early Christian Studies* 7:1 (1999), 83–104.

34. "Round Dance of the Cross," in Acts of John 94.9–95.50.
35. Ibid., 96.1–15.
36. Ibid., 95.27–30.
37. Ibid., 88.12–18.
38. Ibid., 90.1–17.
39. Apocryphon of John 1.5–17; see the recent edition already cited, edited by Frederick Wisse and Michael Waldstein; see also the commentary on the Apocryphon of John by Karen King, forthcoming from Harvard University Press in spring 2003.
40. Apocryphon of John, 1.18–33.
41. Ibid., 2.9–14.
42. Ibid., 2.3–10.
43. The latter part of the citation follows BG 25.14–20; cf. John 1:1–4:10.
44. For our purpose here, the precise identity of the author is not the central point—especially because it is not known. We note, however, that Christoph Markschies has persuasively challenged the traditional identification in his important article "New Research on Ptolemaeus Gnosticus," in Zeitschrift für Antike und Christentum 4 (Berlin and New York, 2000), 249–254.
45. Irenaeus, AH 1.8.5.
46. Ibid., 1.9.1.
47. Ibid., 1.9.2.
48. Ibid., 1.18.1.
49. Ibid., 1.9.4.
50. Ibid., 1.10.1.
51. The question of baptismal practice among Valentinian Christians has provoked considerable debate; for discussion and references, and for a fuller discussion of what is briefly summarized in this chapter, see Pagels, "Ritual in the Gospel of Philip." For a differ-

ent viewpoint, see Einar Thomassons's recent studies of Valentinian practice; for example, his article "How Valentinian Is the Gospel of Philip?" in Turner and McGuire, *Nag Hammadi Library After Fifty Years*, 251–279; and Martha Lee Turner, "On the Coherence of the *Gospel According to Philip*," 223–250. See also the excellent and detailed study by Peter Lampe, *Die stadtrömischen Christen in den ersten beiden Jahrhunderten: Untersuchungen zur Sozialgeschichte* (Tübingen, 1989).

52. Cf. John 3:5; Gospel of Philip 69.4–6, in NHL 141.

53. Gospel of Philip 64.22–26, in NHL 139.

54. Ibid., 64.29–31, in NHL 139.

55. Ibid., 79.25–31, in NHL 147.

56. Ibid., 55.23–24, in NHL 147.

57. Ibid., 71.3–15, in NHL 143.

58. Ibid., 52.21–24, in NHL 132.

59. Ibid., 55.30, in NHL 134.

60. Ibid., 56.26–57.23, in NHL 134–135; for a fuller exposition of the text, see Pagels, "Ritual in the Gospel of Philip."

61. Gospel of Philip, 57.4–6, in NHL 134.

62. Ibid., 67.26–27, in NHL 140.

63. Irenaeus, AH 1.9.4; 1.10.1.

64. Ibid., 3.15.2.

65. Ibid., 1.10.2.

66. Eusebius, *Historia Ecclesiae* 5.23–26.

67. Irenaeus, AH 1.11.9; however, we cannot be certain that the Gospel of Truth that Irenaeus mentions here, and ascribes to "Valentinians," is the same as the text by that name discovered at Nag Hammadi.

68. Ibid., 1.29.4; most scholars regard the teaching Irenaeus summarizes in AH 1.29.1–4 as a paraphrase of the kind of teaching given in the Apocryphon of John.

69. For a much fuller discussion and references, see Pagels, "Irenaeus, the 'Canon of Truth' and the Gospel of John."

70. Irenaeus, AH 1.15.2; Tertullian describes similar behavior, but he may be drawing his account from Irenaeus's writings rather than his own encounters with such teachers, in *Adversus Valentinianos* 1–2; however, passages from Tertullian's polemic, especially, for example, in chapter 4, do recall his keen ear for actual dialogue.

71. Mark 1:7–8; Matthew 3:11; Luke 3:16.

72. Mark 10:38.

73. Galatians 4:5–7.

74. Gospel of Truth 43.5–8, in NHL 49.

75. "Round Dance of the Cross," in Acts of John 96.2–8.

76. Irenaeus, AH 1.21.1.

77. Ibid., 1.21.3.

78. Ibid.; cf. Colossians 3:3.

79. Irenaeus, AH 1.21.3.

80. Ibid., 1.21.4.

81. Gospel of Thomas 50, in NHL 123.

82. Irenaeus, AH 1.21.4.

83. Ibid., 4.33.7.

84. Ibid., 1.21.1.

CHAPTER FIVE: CONSTANTINE AND THE CATHOLIC CHURCH

1. Irenaeus, AH 2.13.8.

2. Ibid., 2.13.10.

3. Ibid., 2.13.3; 2.13.10. For discussion, see Pagels, "Irenaeus, the 'Canon of Truth' and the Gospel of John."

4. Irenaeus, AH 3.19.2.

5. Ibid., 3.19.1.

6. John 20:20–28; cited in Irenaeus, AH 5.7.1.

7. Irenaeus, AH 5.1.1.

8. Ibid.

9. Ibid., 1.20.1.

10. The question of canon and its introduction into Christian tradi-

tion is a difficult and disputed one. A. C. Sundberg, in "Canon Muratori: A Fourth Century List," *Harvard Theological Review* 66 (1968), 1–41, offers an incisive critique of the traditional second-century dating of the Muratorian canon list, previously believed to be the earliest known list of the New Testament writings. For a careful and persuasive discussion, see Hahneman, *Muratorian Fragment*. For an excellent and measured review of the question, see Harold Gamble, *The New Testament Canon: Its Making and Meaning* (Minneapolis, 1985); and "The New Testament Canon: Recent Research and the *Status Quaestionis*," a forthcoming article which he kindly allowed me to read in manuscript. For an outstanding introduction to issues in the formation of the New Testament, see David E. Aune, *The New Testament in Its Literary Environment* (Philadelphia, 1987). See also the incisive study by Franz Stuhlhofer, *Der Gebrauch der Bibel von Jesus bis Euseb: Eine stätistische Untersuchung zur Kanonsgeschichte* (Wuppertal, 1988); also John Barton, *People of the Book? The Authority of the Bible in Christianity* (Louisville, Ky., 1989).

11. Irenaeus, AH 1.9.4. For discussion, see the classic discussion of "canon" as baptismal confession by Adolf von Harnack, in *History of Dogma*, volume I, chapter 3; also the critique by R. Seeberg in *Lehrbuch der Dogmengeschichte* I–II (Basel, 1953–54), as well as the incisive discussion by D. van den Eynde, "Les Normes de l'Enseignement Chrétien dans la littérature patristique des trois premiers siècles," in J. Duculot, ed., *Ecriture et Tradition*, Catholic University of Louvain, Dissertation Series 2.25 (Paris, 1933), 281–313; also L. William Countryman, "Tertullian and the *Regula Fidei*," *The Second Century* 2 (1982), 201–227.

12. Irenaeus, AH 3.11.7.

13. Scholars have debated the transmission history of John's gospel in sources preceding Irenaeus; see, for example, the discussion in Koester, *Ancient Christian Gospels*, 240–267. In an earlier discussion, Professor Koester apparently agreed with many others that Justin

had alluded to John or Johannine tradition when he apparently alluded to John 3:5 in his description of baptism (I *Apology* 61). But in his more recent book, Koester evaluates Justin's version of this saying as an early, independently transmitted tradition (361). On manuscript evidence for the Johannine gospel in Egypt, see Colin H. Roberts, *Manuscript, Society, and Belief in Early Christian Egypt* (London, 1979). T. E. Pollard, *Johannine Christology and the Early Church,* says that Theophilus of Antioch is the first Christian writer to attribute the fourth gospel to "John," and "to quote explicitly from the fourth gospel" (40). See also the important studies by J. N. Sanders, *The Fourth Gospel in the Early Church* (Cambridge, 1943), and Maurice F. Wiles, *Spiritual Gospel.*

14. See the later recensions of Ignatius's letters for apparent insertions of Johannine material.

15. For references, see Chapter 3, note 40; also Trevett, *Montanism,* 139–140; see also Charles H. Cosgrove, "Justin Martyr and the Emerging Christian Community," *Vigiliae Christianae* 36 (1982), 209–232.

16. Irenaeus writes that he had heard from Polycarp that John, "the disciple of the Lord," was the archenemy of Cerinthus, whom, he said, John had pronounced "the firstborn of Satan" (AH 3.3.4).

17. For recent discussion, see, for example, T. Baarda, "Diaphonia– Symphonia: Factors in the Harmonization of the Gospels, Especially in the Diatessaron of Tatian," in W. L. Peterson, ed., *Gospel Traditions in the Second Century: Origins, Recensions, Text, and Transmission* (Notre Dame, 1989), 133–154; and the recent study by W. L. Peterson, *Tatian's Diatessaron: Its Creation, Dissemination, Significance, and History in Scholarship* (Leiden, 1994).

18. Irenaeus, AH 3.11.1; 3.3.4; Irenaeus indicates that Ptolemy's disciples agree (1.8.5).

19. Ibid., 3.11.8–9. As T. C. Skeat writes in "Irenaeus and the Four-Gospel Canon," *Novum Testamentum* 34 (1992), 194: "Every study of the Canon of the Four Gospels begins, and rightly begins, with

the famous passage in which Irenaeus, writing about the year
185, seeks to defend the Canon by finding a mystical significance
in the number four."

20. Irenaeus, AH 3.11.8–9.

21. Irenaeus quotes a written commentary on the Johannine Prologue in 1.8.5. Although he suggests that what follows is the
teaching of Valentinus's disciple Ptolemy, it is more likely a writing by one of Ptolemy's disciples; see Markschies, "New Research
on Ptolemaeus Gnosticus," 249–254. See also Pasquier, "Interpretation of the Prologue," 484–498.

22. Irenaeus, AH 1.9.2–3.

23. Thanks to Paula Fredriksen for reminding me that this inference
is not what Irenaeus, obviously influenced by Middle Platonic
thinking, would have been likely to understand.

24. For fuller discussion of the prologue translations, see Pagels, "Exegesis of Genesis 1," 208–209, and Dodd, *Interpretation of the Fourth
Gospel*, 268–269. Many English translations, such as, for example the Revised Standard Version, edited by Herbert G. May and
Bruce M. Metzger, not only capitalize the term *logos* (word) but
also translate the pronouns in 1:7–10 as "he," as if they referred
to *Jesus Christ*, instead of indicating that the Greek can be read
as neuter or masculine, depending on whether one reads the
pronouns' antecedent as *phos* ("light," neuter in Greek) or *logos*
("word," masculine in Greek). Even the reader who goes back to
the Greek original may find, as, for example, in the edition by
Nestle-Aland, that the Greek text actually capitalizes the term
logos, which, in the early manuscripts, would have been indistin-
guishable from the rest of the text.

25. Irenaeus, AH 1.22.1.

26. Ibid., 4.20.1–10.

27. Ibid., 4.20.10–11.

28. Ibid., 5.15.2.

29. Ibid., 3.11.8. "Matthew, too, relates [Christ's] human generation, saying (Matthew 1:1) . . ."

30. Ibid. "The gospel according to Luke . . . takes up his priestly character."

31. Ibid. "Mark, on the other hand, begins with the prophetic spirit descending from on high" (cf. Mark 1:1).

32. Ibid., 3.11.1.

33. Ibid., 4.7.4.

34. Ibid., 4.18.4.

35. Ibid., 17.4–6.

36. Ibid., 4.18.1–4.

37. A. S. Jacobs, "The Disorder of Books: Priscillian's Canonical Defense of Apocrypha," *Harvard Theological Review* 93:2 (2000), 135–159; see also A. Reed, "Apocrypha, 'Outside Books,' and Pseudepigrapha: Ancient Categories and Modern Perceptions of Parabiblical Literature," paper presented at the Philadelphia Seminar on Christian Origins: Parabiblical Literature, October 10, 2002.

38. Irenaeus, AH 4.36.2–4.

39. Ibid., 5.2.1–2.

40. Ibid., 5.21–34.

41. Ibid., 1, *Praefatio.*

42. See the recent and detailed study by Christoph Markschies, *Valentinus Gnosticus?*; also Lampe, *Die stadtrömischen Christen in den ersten beiden Jahrhunderten,* 251–268.

43. See, for example, Judith Kovacs, "Echoes of Valentinian Exegesis in Clement of Alexander and Origen," paper given at Pisa, August 2000, forthcoming in *Origeniana Octava.*

44. Tertullian, *Prescription Against Heretics* 3.

45. For an incisive and intriguing discussion of correlated fourth-century phenomena, see David Brakke, *Athanasius and the Politics of Asceticism* (Oxford and New York, 1995).

46. Tertullian, *Against the Valentinians* 4.

47. Tertullian, *Prescription Against Heretics* 41.
48. Irenaeus, AH 3.15.2.
49. Exodus 9:35; Irenaeus, AH 4.28.3–30.
50. Genesis 19:33–35; Irenaeus, AH 4.31.1–3.
51. William James, *The Varieties of Religious Experience* (Cambridge, Mass., 1985).
52. John 4:46–53.
53. John 4:11–23; for the fragments that remain from Heracleon's commentary, see Werner Foerster, *Gnosis, Die Fragments Heracleons* (Zürich, 1971), 63–86. For discussion of these fragments, see Pagels, *Johannine Gospel in Gnostic Exegesis;* and more recently the study by J. M. Poffet, *La méthode exégétique d'Héracléon et d'Origène* (Fribourg, 1985).
54. John 4:16.
55. Heracleon, Fragment 19, in Origen's *Commentary on John* 13.15.
56. John 4:23, see Heracleon, Fragments 23–25, in Origen, *Commentary on John* 13.19. For an incisive discussion of "gnostic" views of worship, see Klaus Koschorke, *Die Polemik der Gnostiker gegen das kirchliche Christentum* (Leiden, 1978), especially 142–147.
57. See the edition and translation by Frederick Wisse and Michael Waldstein, *Apocryphon of John: Synopsis of Nag Hammadi Codices II.1; III, 1; and IV.1, with BG 8502, 2,* also the fascinating essay by Waldstein, "The Primal Triad in the *Apocryphon of John*," in Turner and McGuire, *Nag Hammadi Library After Fifty Years,* 154–187, and the commentary forthcoming by Karen King from Harvard University Press.
58. Apocryphon of John 20.15–25, in NHL 110.
59. For this version of the story, see On the Origin of the World, 108–118, in NHL 167–174.
60. Apocryphon of John 26.14–15, in NHL 113.
61. Ibid., 26.15–19, in NHL 113.
62. I Corinthians 13:12.

63. Apocryphon of John 30.2–4, in NHL 115.

64. Ibid., 11.20–21, in NHL 105.

65. Genesis 3:16–19.

66. Genesis 3:16 b.

67. Genesis 3:22–24.

68. Apocryphon of John 28.5–30.11, in NHL 114–115.

69. Irenaeus, AH 4.19.2.

70. Eusebius, *Vita Constantinae* 1.26–29.

71. Eusebius, *Historia Ecclesiae* 10.6.

72. Ibid., 10.5.15–17.

73. For a detailed account, see Timothy D. Barnes, *Constantine and Eusebius* (Cambridge and London, 1981), especially 208–227.

74. Eusebius, *Historia Ecclesiae* 10.7.

75. *Codex Theodosius* 19.5.1.

76. For a forthcoming article that suggests Constantine was *not* the emperor who built the first basilica of St. Peter on the Vatican (as tradition holds), see Glen Bowersock, in the supplement to *Antiquite Tardive* in honor of Lellia Cracco Ruggini, and also in a forthcoming Cambridge University Press volume on the Vatican, edited by William Tronzo.

77. Eusebius, *Vita Constantinae* 2.45–46. See Ramsay MacMullen, *Christianizing the Roman Empire, A.D. 100–400* (New Haven and London, 1884), 43–59; also Barnes, *Constantine and Eusebius*, especially 224–260.

78. On the subsidies of grain, see M. J. Hollerich, "The Alexandrian Bishops and the Grain Trade: Ecclesiastical Commerce in Late Roman Egypt," *Journal of the Economic and Social History of the Orient* 25 (1982), 187–207.

79. Barnes, *Constantine and Eusebius*, 252.

80. Ibid., 252; *Codex Theodosius*, 16.8.6; 16.8.1.

81. The sketch presented here is owed primarily to the careful historiography of Timothy D. Barnes, who has published several

fine histories of this period. Besides his book *Constantine and Eusebius*, see his more recent *Athanasius and Constantius: Theology and Politics in the Constantinian Empire* (Cambridge and London, 1993). An excellent article that presents an overview of these developments is Glen W. Bowersock, "From Emperor to Bishop: The Self-Conscious Transformation of Political Power in the Fourth Century A.D.," *Classical Philology* 81 (1986), 298–302; see also the important work of Peter Brown, including *Power and Persuasion in Late Antiquity: Towards a Christian Empire* (Madison, Wis., 1992), and *Authority and the Sacred: Aspects of the Christianisation of the Roman World* (Cambridge, 1995); Susannah Elm, *Virgins of God: The Making of Asceticism in Late Antiquity* (Oxford and New York, 1992); and David Brakke, *Athanasius and the Politics of Asceticism.*

82. Glen W. Bowersock offers an excellent survey of these events in "From Emperor to Bishop."

83. Letter, cited in J. Stevenson, *A New Eusebius: Documents Illustrative of the History of the Church to A.D. 337* (London, 1957), 358.

84. Eusebius, *Vita Constantinae* 4.24.

85. Barnes, *Constantine and Eusebius.*

86. Letter of Eusebius of Caesarea to his church, in Socrates' *Historia Ecclesiae* 1.8. For a thoughtful and balanced discussion, see Rowan Williams, *Arius: Heresy and Tradition* (London, 1987).

87. Barnes, *Constantine and Eusebius*, 215.

88. See MacMullen, *Christianizing the Roman Empire*, 59–119; see also Stark, *Rise of Christianity.*

89. See Virginia Burrus, *The Making of a Heretic: Gender, Authority, and the Priscillianist Controversy* (Berkeley, 1998), for a fascinating example of the persistence of groups that catholic Christians regarded as deviant.

90. Barnes, *Constantine and Eusebius*, 213.

91. Erik Peterson, *Monotheismus als politisches problem: ein beitrag zur geschichte der politischen theologie im Imperium romanum* (Leipzig, 1935), later interpreted by George H. Williams, "Christology and Church-

State Relations in the Fourth Century," in two installments in *Church History* 20:4 (1951), 3–33, and 20:4 (1951), 3–33.

92. For an incisive discussion of the evidence, see Susannah Elm, *Virgins of God: The Making of Asceticism in Late Antiquity* (Oxford and New York, 1992).

93. See Philip Rousseau, *Pachomius in the Age of Jerome and Cassian* (Oxford, 1978), and his important book *Ascetics, Authority, and the Church: The Making of a Community in Fourth-Century Egypt* (Berkeley, Los Angeles, and London, 1985); Peter Brown, *Society and the Holy* (London and New York, 1982), and *Power, Politics, and Persuasion;* David Brakke, *Athanasius and the Politics of Asceticism;* Birger A. Pearson and James E. Goerhing, *The Roots of Egyptian Christianity* (Philadelphia, 1980), and *The Making of a Church in Fourth-Century Egypt* (Berkeley, 1985); and Samuel Rubenson, *The Letters of St. Anthony: Origenist Theology, Monastic Tradition, and the Making of a Saint* (Lund, 1990); see also Richard Valentasis, *Spiritual Guides of the Third Century: A Semiotic Study of the Guide-Disciple Relationship in Christianity, Neoplatonism, Hermetism, and Gnosticism* (Minneapolis, 1991).

94. Athanasius, *Festal Letter* 39. For discussion, see, for example, Martin Tetz, "Athanasius und die Einheit der Kirche: Zur ökumenisches Bedeutung eines Kirchenväters," *Zeitschrift für Theologie und Kirche* 81 (1984), 205–207; and Brakke, "Canon Formation and Social Conflict."

95. On Athanasius's use of the term *dianoia* as the standard for exegesis, see T. E. Pollard, "The Exegesis of Scripture and the Arian Controversy," in *The John Rylands Library* 41 (1958–59), 421–429; as in Athanasius, *Or. Contra Ar.* 7 (PG 261); also C. Kannengiesser, *Arius and Athanasius: Two Alexandrian Theologians* (Aldershot, Hampshire, Great Britain, and Brookfield, Vt., 1991).

96. Augustine, *On the Incarnation of the Word* 6:1; 13.2; 10.3; see also 11.3. God "gives [humanity] a share in His own image, our Lord Jesus Christ, and makes them according to His own image and after His likeness, so that, by such grace perceiving the

image, that is, the Word of the Father, they may be able through Him to . . . know their Master and live the happy and blessed life."

97. MacMullen, *Christianizing the Roman Empire*, 86; on the advantages of conversion after that time, see "Nonreligious Factors in Conversion," 52–59; see also Stark, *Rise of Christianity*.

98. I find persuasive the arguments of Timothy D. Barnes, in *Constantine and Eusebius*, 208–260; "The Constantinian Reformation," Crake Lectures, 1982 (Sackville, 1986); and "The Constantinian Settlement," in *Eusebius, Judaism, and Christianity* (Detroit, 1992), 655–657.

99. Jacob Burckhardt's classic book suggests the traditional view; see also Eduard Schwartz, *Zur Geschichte des Athanasius* (Berlin, 1959), *Kaiser Constantin und die christliche Kirche* (Leipzig, 1936), and *Zeit Constantins des Grosses* (Leipzig, 1880).

100. See, for example, Brown, *Power and Persuasion*; Richard Lim, *Public Disputation, Power, and Social Order in Late Antiquity* (Berkeley, 1995); Averill Cameron, *Christianity and the Rhetoric of Empire* (Berkeley, Los Angeles, and Oxford, 1991); and Virginia Burrus, *"Begotten, Not Made": Conceiving Manhood in Late Antiquity* (Stanford, 2000).

101. I am grateful to my friend and colleague Heinrich von Staden for raising this point; for discussion of "the dynamics of faith" in terms of Christian theology, see, for example, Paul Tillich, *The Dynamics of Faith* (New York, 1957). For a Buddhist (and thus non-theistic) view, see Sharon Saltzberg, *Faith: Trusting Your Own Deepest Experience* (New York, 2002).

102. Tertullian, *Against the Valentinians* 4.

103. Peter Berger, *The Heretical Imperative: Contemporary Possibilities of Religious Affirmation* (New York, 1979).

104. Matthew 7:7; note Tertullian's objections to the way that "heretics" use this saying (much as I have here) in his *Prescription Against Heretics* 8–13.

THE GOSPEL OF THOMAS

꜀ʘʘʘꜜ

This text is adapted by Elaine Pagels and Marvin Meyer from Professor Meyer's translation in *The Secret Teachings of Jesus* (Random House), in consultation with the Scholars Version published in *The Complete Gospels* (Polebridge Press).

These are the secret sayings that the living Jesus spoke and Judas Thomas the Twin wrote down.

1 And he said, "Whoever finds the interpretation of these sayings will not taste death."

2 Jesus said, "Let one who seeks not stop seeking until he finds. When he finds, he will be troubled. When he is troubled, he will be astonished and will rule over all."

3 Jesus said, "If your leaders say to you, 'Look, the Kingdom is in heaven,' then the birds of heaven will precede you. If they say to you, 'It is in the sea,' then the fish will precede you. Rather, the Kingdom is inside you and outside you. When you know yourselves, then you will be known, and you will understand that you are children of the living Father. But if you do not know yourselves, then you live in poverty, and you are poverty."

4 Jesus said, "The man old in days will not hesitate to ask a little child seven days old about the place of life, and that person will live. For many of the first will be last and will become a single one."

5 Jesus said, "Recognize what is before your eyes, and the mysteries will be revealed to you. For there is nothing hidden that will not be revealed."

6 His disciples asked him and said to him, "Do you want us to fast?

How should we pray? Should we give alms? What diet should we observe?"

Jesus said, "Do not tell lies, and do not do what you hate, because all things are revealed before heaven. For there is nothing hidden that will not be revealed, and there is nothing covered up that will not be uncovered."

7 Jesus said, "Blessed is the lion that the human will eat, so that the lion becomes human. Cursed is the human that the lion will eat, and the lion will become human."

8 And he said, "The man is like a wise fisherman who cast his net into the sea and drew it up from the sea full of little fish. Among them the wise fisherman discovered a fine big fish. So the fisherman threw all the little fish back into the sea and with no hesitation kept the big fish. Whoever has ears to hear, let him hear!"

9 Jesus said,

Look, the sower went out, took a handful [of seeds], and scattered them. Some fell on the road, and the birds came and gathered them. Others fell on rock, and they did not take root in the soil or produce any heads of grain. Others fell among the thorns, and the thorns choked the seeds and worms consumed them. Still others fell on good soil, and it brought forth a good crop: it yielded sixty per measure and one hundred twenty per measure.

10 Jesus said, "I have cast fire upon the world, and look, I am guarding it until it blazes."

11 Jesus said, "This heaven will pass away, and the one above it will pass away. The dead are not alive, and the living will not die. During the days when you ate what is dead, you made it alive. When you are in the light, what will you do? On the day when you were one, you became two. But when you become two, what will you do?"

12 The disciples said to Jesus, "We know that you are going to leave us. Who is going to be our leader then?"

Jesus said to them, "Wherever you are, you are to go to James the Just, for whose sake heaven and earth came into being."

13 Jesus said to his disciples, "Compare me to someone and tell me whom I am like."

Simon Peter said to him, "You are like a righteous messenger."

Matthew said to him, "You are like a wise philosopher."

Thomas said to him, "Master, my mouth is utterly unable to say what you are like."

Jesus said, "I am not your master. Because you have drunk, you have become intoxicated from the bubbling spring that I have tended."

And he took him, and withdrew, and spoke three sayings to him.

When Thomas came back to his companions, they asked him, "What did Jesus say to you?"

Thomas said to them, "If I tell you even one of the sayings he spoke to me, you will pick up rocks and stone me. Then fire will come forth from the rocks and devour you."

14 Jesus said to them, "If you fast, you will bring sin upon your-selves. If you pray, you will be condemned. If you give alms, you will harm your spirits. When you go into any country and wander around from place to place, and the people receive you, eat what they serve you and heal the sick among them. For what goes into your mouth will not defile you; rather, it is what comes out of your mouth that will defile you."

15 Jesus said, "When you see one who was not born of woman, bow down and worship. That one is your Father."

16 Jesus said, "Perhaps people think that I have come to cast peace upon the world. They do not know that I have come to cast strife upon the earth: fire, sword, war. For there will be five in a house: there will be three against two and two against three, father against son and son against father, and they will stand solitary."

17 Jesus said, "I shall give you what no eye has seen, what no ear has heard, what no hand has touched, what has never arisen in a human heart."

18 The disciples said to Jesus, "Tell us about the end."

Jesus said, "Have you already found the beginning, then, that you seek for the end? For where the beginning is the end will be. Blessed is the one who stands at the beginning: that one will know the end and will not taste death."

19 Jesus said, "Blessed is the one who came into being before coming into being. If you become my disciples and listen to my sayings, these stones will serve you. For there are five trees in Paradise for you; they do not change, summer or winter, and their leaves do not fall. Whoever knows them will not taste death."

20 The disciples said to Jesus, "Tell us what the Kingdom of Heaven is like."

He said to them,

It is like a mustard seed. [It] is the smallest of all seeds, but when it falls on prepared soil, it grows into a large plant and shelters the birds of heaven.

21 Mary said to Jesus, "What are your disciples like?"
He said,

They are like little children living in a field that is not theirs. When the owners of the field come, they will say, "Give us back our field." They take off their clothes in front of them in order to give it back to them, and they return their field to them. For this reason I say, if the owners of a house know that a thief is coming, they will be on guard before the thief arrives, and will not let the thief break into their house of their domain and steal their possessions. As for you, then, be on guard against the world. Prepare yourselves with great strength, so the robbers cannot find a way to get to you, for the trouble you expect will come. Let there be among you a person who understands. When the crop ripened, he came quickly carrying a sickle and harvested it. Whoever has ears to hear, let him hear!

22 Jesus saw some babies nursing. He said to his disciples, "These nursing babies are like those who enter the Kingdom."

They said to him, "Then shall we enter the Kingdom as babies?"

Jesus said to them, "When you make the two into one, and when you make the inner like the outer and the outer like the inner, and the upper like the lower, and when you make male and female into a single one, so that the male will not be male nor the female be female, when you make eyes in place of an eye, a hand in place of a hand, a foot in place of a foot, an image in place of an image, then you will enter [the Kingdom]."

23 Jesus said, "I shall choose you, one from a thousand and two from ten thousand, and they will stand as a single one."

24 His disciples said, "Show us the place where you are, for we must seek it."

He said to them, "Whoever has ears to hear, let him hear! There is light within a person of light, and it lights up the whole world. If it does not shine, it is dark."

25 Jesus said, "Love your brother like your soul; protect him like the pupil of your eye."

26 Jesus said, "You see the sliver in your brother's eye, but you do not see the timber in your own eye. When you take the timber out of your own eye, then you will see well enough to remove the sliver from your brother's eye.

27 "If you do not fast from the world, you will not find the Kingdom. If you do not observe the sabbath day as a sabbath day, you will not see the Father."

28 Jesus said, "I took my stand in the midst of the world, and in flesh I appeared to them. I found them all drunk, and I did not find any of them thirsty. My soul ached for the children of humanity, because they are blind in their hearts and do not see, for they came into the world empty, and they also seek to depart from the world empty. But meanwhile they are drunk. When they shake off their wine, then they will repent."

29 Jesus said, "If the flesh came into being because of spirit, that is a marvel, but if spirit came into being because of the body, that is a marvel of marvels. Yet I marvel at how this great wealth has come to dwell in this poverty."

30 Jesus said, "Where there are three deities, they are divine. Where there are two or one, I am with that one."

31 Jesus said, "No prophet is welcome in his own village; no physician cures those who know him."

32 Jesus said, "A city built on a high hill and fortified cannot fall, nor can it be hidden."

33 Jesus said, "What you will hear in your ear, in the other ear proclaim from your rooftops. For no one lights a lamp and puts it under a basket, nor does one put it in a hidden place. Rather, one puts it on a lampstand so that all who come and go will see its light."

34 Jesus said, "If a blind person leads a blind person, both of them will fall into a hole."

35 Jesus said, "One cannot enter a strong man's house and take it by force without binding his hands. Then one can loot his house."

36 Jesus said, "Do not worry, from morning to evening and from evening to morning, about what you are going to wear."

37 His disciples said, "When will you appear to us and when shall we see you?"

Jesus said, "When you strip off your clothes without being ashamed, and you take your clothes and put them under your feet like little children and trample them, then [you] will see the son of the living one and you will not be afraid."

38 Jesus said, "Often you have desired to hear these sayings that I am speaking to you, and you have no one else from whom to hear them. There will be days when you will seek me and you will not find me."

39 Jesus said, "The Pharisees and the scholars have taken the keys of knowledge and have hidden them. They have not entered, nor have they allowed those who want to enter to do so. As for you, be as wise as serpents and as innocent as doves."

40 Jesus said, "A grapevine has been planted apart from the Father. Since it is not strong, it will be pulled up by its root and will perish."

41 Jesus said, "Those who have something in hand will be given more, and those who have nothing will be deprived of even the little they have."

42 Jesus said, "Become passersby."

43 His disciples said to him, "Who are you to say these things to us?"

"You do not understand who I am from what I say to you. Rather, you have become like the Jewish people, for they love the tree but hate its fruit, or they love the fruit but hate the tree."

44 Jesus said, "Whoever blasphemes against the Father will be forgiven, and whoever blasphemes against the son will be forgiven, but whoever blasphemes against the holy spirit will not be forgiven, either on earth or in heaven."

45 Jesus said, "Grapes are not harvested from thorn trees, nor are figs gathered from thistles, for they yield no fruit. Good persons produce good from what they have stored up; bad persons produce evil from the wickedness they have stored up in their hearts, and say evil things. For from the overflow of the heart they bring forth evil."

46 Jesus said, "From Adam to John the Baptist, among those born of women, no one is so much greater than John the Baptist that his eyes should not be averted. But I have said that whoever among you becomes a child will know the Kingdom and will become greater than John."

47 Jesus said, "A person cannot mount two horses or bend two bows, and a servant cannot serve two masters, otherwise that servant will honor the one and offend the other. No one drinks aged wine and immediately wants to drink new wine. New wine is not poured into old wineskins, or they might break, and aged wine is not poured into a new wineskin, or it might spoil. An old patch is not sewn onto a new garment, since it would create a tear."

48 Jesus said, "If two make peace with each other in a single house, they will say to the mountain, 'Move from here!' and it will move."

49 Jesus said, "Blessed are those who are solitary and chosen, for you will find the Kingdom. For you have come from it, and you will return there again."

50 Jesus said, "If they say to you, 'Where have you come from?' say to them, 'We have come from the light, from the place where the light came into being by itself, established [itself], and appeared in their image.' If they say to you, 'Who are you?' say, 'We are its children, and we are the chosen of the living Father.' If they ask you, 'What is the sign of your Father in you?' say to them, 'It is movement and rest.'"

51 His disciples said to him, "When will the rest for the dead take place, and when will the new world come?"

He said to them, "What you look forward to has already come, but you do not recognize it."

52 His disciples said to him, "Twenty-four prophets have spoken in Israel, and they all spoke of you."

He said to them, "You have disregarded the living one who is in your presence and have spoken of the dead."

53 His disciples said to him, "Is circumcision beneficial or not?"

He said to them, "If it were beneficial, their father would produce children already circumcised from their mother. Rather, the true circumcision in spirit has become profitable in every respect."

54 Jesus said, "Blessed are the poor, for yours is the Kingdom of Heaven."

55 Jesus said, "Whoever does not hate father and mother cannot be my disciple, and whoever does not hate brothers and sisters, and carry the cross as I do, will not be worthy of me."

56 Jesus said, "Whoever has come to know the world has discovered a carcass, and whoever has discovered a carcass, of that person the world is not worthy."

57 Jesus said,

> The Kingdom of the Father is like a person who had [good] seed. His enemy came during the night and sowed weeds among the good seed. The man did not let the workers pull up the weeds, but said to them, "No, otherwise you might go to pull up the weeds and pull up the wheat along with them." For on the day of the harvest the weeds will be conspicuous and will be pulled up and burned.

58 Jesus said, "Blessed is the one who has suffered and has found life."

59 Jesus said, "Look to the living one as long as you live, otherwise you might die and then try to see the living one, and you will be unable to see."

60 [He saw] a Samaritan carrying a lamb as he was going to Judea. He said to his disciples, "[Why is] that person [carrying] the lamb around?"

They said to him, "So that he may kill it and eat it."

He said to them, "He will not eat it while it is alive, but only after he has killed it and it has become a carcass."

They said, "Otherwise he cannot do it."

He said to them, "So also with you, seek a place of rest for yourselves, lest you become a carcass and be eaten."

61 Jesus said, "Two will recline on a couch; one will die, one will live."

Salome said, "Who are you, man? You have climbed onto my couch and eaten from my table as if from one."

Jesus said to her, "I am the one who comes from what is undivided. I was granted from the things of my Father."

[Salome said,] "I am your disciple."

[Jesus said,] "For this reason I say, whoever is [undivided] will be full of light, but whoever is divided will be full of darkness."

62 Jesus said, "I disclose my mysteries to those [who are worthy] of [my] mysteries. Do not let your left hand know what your right hand is doing."

63 Jesus said,

There was a rich man who had a great deal of money. He said, "I shall invest my money so that I may sow, reap, plant, and fill my storehouses with produce, that I may lack nothing." These were the things he was thinking in his heart, but that very night he died. Whoever has ears to hear, let him hear!

64 Jesus said,

A man was receiving guests. When he had prepared the dinner, he sent his servant to invite the guests. The servant went

to the first and said, "My master invites you." The first replied, "Some merchants owe me money; they are coming to
me tonight. I have to go and give them instructions. Please
excuse me from dinner." The servant went to another and
said, "My master has invited you." The second said to the
servant, "I have bought a house, and I have been called away
for a day. I shall have no time." The servant went to another
and said, "My master invites you." The third said to the servant, "My friend is to be married, and I am to arrange the
banquet. I shall not be able to come. Please excuse me from
dinner." The servant went to another and said, "My master
invites you." The fourth said to the servant, "I have bought
an estate, and I am going to collect the rent. I shall not be
able to come. Please excuse me." The servant returned and
said to his master, "Those whom you invited to dinner have
asked to be excused." The master said to his servant, "Go out
on the streets and bring back whomever you find to come to
dinner."

"Buyers and merchants [will] not enter the places of my Father."

65 He said,

A [usurer] owned a vineyard and rented it to some farmers, so they could work it and he could collect its produce from them. He sent his servant so the farmers would
give him the produce from the vineyard. They seized him,
beat him, and almost killed him, and the servant returned
and told his master. His master said, "Perhaps he did not
know them." He sent another servant, and the farmers beat
that one as well. Then the master sent his son and said, "Perhaps they will show my son some respect." Because the
farmers knew that he was the heir to the vineyard, they
seized him and killed him. Whoever has ears to hear, let him
hear!

66 Jesus said, "Show me the stone that the builders rejected: that is the cornerstone."

67 Jesus said, "Whoever knows everything, but is lacking within, lacks everything."

68 Jesus said, "Blessed are you when you are hated and persecuted; wherever you have been persecuted, no place will be found."

69 Jesus said, "Blessed are those who have been persecuted in their hearts: they are the ones who have truly come to know the Father. Blessed are those who hunger, that the belly of the one in need may be filled."

70 Jesus said, "If you bring forth what is within you, what you have will save you. If you do not have that within you, what you do not have within you [will] destroy you."

71 Jesus said, "I shall destroy [this] house, and no one will be able to build it [again]."

72 A [person said] to him, "Tell my brothers to divide my father's possessions with me."

He said to the person, "Man, who made me a divider?"

He turned to his disciples and said to them, "I am not a divider, am I?"

73 Jesus said, "The harvest is great but the workers are few, so ask the master of the harvest to send workers to the fields."

74 Someone said, "Lord, there are many around the drinking trough, but there is nothing in the well."

75 Jesus said, "There are many standing at the door, but only those who are solitary will enter the bridal chamber."

76 Jesus said,

The Kingdom of the Father is like a merchant who had a supply of merchandise and then found a pearl. That merchant was prudent; he sold the merchandise and bought the single pearl for himself.

"So also with you, seek his treasure that is unfailing, that is enduring, where no moth comes to eat and no worm destroys."

77 Jesus said, "I am the light that is over all things. I am all. From me all came forth, and to me all extends. Split a piece of wood, and I am there. Lift up the stone, and you will find me there."

78 Jesus said, "Why have you come out to the countryside? To see a reed shaken by the wind? And to see a person dressed in fine clothing, [like your] rulers and your powerful men? They are dressed in fine clothing, and they cannot understand truth."

79 A woman in the crowd said to him, "Blessed are the womb that bore you and the breasts that nourished you."

He said to [her], "Blessed are those who have heard the word of the Father and have truly kept it. For there will be days when you will say, 'Blessed are the womb that has not conceived and the breasts that have not given milk.'"

80 Jesus said, "Whoever has come to know the world has discovered the body, and whoever has discovered the body, of that one the world is not worthy."

81 Jesus said, "The one who has become wealthy should reign, and the one who has power should renounce [it]."

82 Jesus said, "Whoever is near me is near the fire, and whoever is far from me is far from the Kingdom."

83 Jesus said, "Images are visible to people, but the light within them is hidden in the image of the Father's light. The Father will be revealed, but his image is hidden by his light."

84 Jesus said, "When you see your likeness [in a mirror], you are pleased. But when you see your images that came into being before you and that neither die nor become visible, how much you will have to bear!"

85 Jesus said, "Adam came from great power and great wealth, but he was not worthy of you. For had he been worthy, [he would] not [have tasted] death."

86 Jesus said, "[Foxes have] their dens and birds have their nests, but the son of man has no place to lie down and rest."

87 Jesus said, "Miserable is the body that depends on a body, and miserable is the soul that depends on these two."

88 Jesus said, "The messengers and the prophets will come to you and give you what belongs to you. You, in turn, give them what you have, and say to yourselves, 'When will they come and take what belongs to them?'"

89 Jesus said, "Why do you wash the outside of the cup? Do you not understand that the one who made the inside is also the one who made the outside?"

90 Jesus said, "Come to me, for my yoke is easy and my rule is gentle, and you will find rest for yourselves."

91 They said to him, "Tell us who you are so that we may believe in you."

He said to them, "You search the face of heaven and earth, but you have not come to know the one who stands before you, and you do not know how to understand the present moment."

92 Jesus said, "Seek and you will find. In the past, however, I did not tell you the things about which you asked me then. Now I am willing to tell them, but you are not seeking them.

93 "Do not give what is holy to dogs, or they might throw them upon the manure pile. Do not throw pearls [to] swine, or they might make [mud] of it."

94 Jesus [said], "One who seeks will find, and for [one who knocks] it will be opened."

95 [Jesus said], "If you have money, do not lend it at interest. Rather, give [it] to someone from whom you will not get it back."

96 Jesus [said], "The Kingdom of the Father is like [a] woman who took a little leaven, [hid] it in dough, and made it into large loaves of bread. Whoever has ears to hear, let him hear!"

97 Jesus said,

> The Kingdom of the [Father] is like a woman who was carrying a [jar] full of meal. While she was walking along [a] distant road, the handle of the jar broke and the meal spilled behind her [along] the road. She did not know it; she noticed no accident. When she reached her house, she put the jar down and discovered that it was empty.

98 Jesus said,

> The Kingdom of the Father is like a person who wanted to kill a powerful man. While still at home he drew his sword and thrust it into the wall to find out whether his hand would go in. Then he killed the powerful man.

99 The disciples said to him, "Your brothers and your mother are standing outside."

He said to them, "Those here who do what my Father wants are my brothers and my mother. They are the ones who will enter the Kingdom of my Father."

100 They showed Jesus a gold coin and said to him, "Caesar's men demand taxes from us."

He said to them, "Give Caesar what belongs to Caesar, give God what belongs to God, and give me what is mine.

101 "Whoever does not hate [father] and mother as I do cannot be my [disciple], and whoever does [not] love [father and] mother as I do cannot be my [disciple]. For my mother [gave me falsehood], but my true [mother] gave me life."

102 Jesus said, "Woe to the Pharisees. For they are like a dog sleeping in the cattle manger: the dog neither eats nor [lets] the cattle eat."

103 Jesus said, "Blessed are those who know where the robbers will enter, so that [they] may prepare, collect their resources, and be ready before the robbers come."

104 They said to Jesus, "Come, let us pray today and let us fast."

Jesus said, "What sin have I committed, or how have I been undone? Rather, when the groom leaves the bridal chamber, then let people fast and pray."

105 Jesus said, "Whoever knows the father and the mother will be called the child of a whore."

106 Jesus said, "When you make the two into one, you will become children of humanity, and when you say, 'Mountain, move from here!' it will move."

107 Jesus said,

> The Kingdom is like a shepherd who had a hundred sheep. One of them, the largest, went astray. He left the ninety-nine and looked for the one until he found it. After his toil, he said to the sheep, "I love you more than the ninety-nine."

108 Jesus said, "Whoever drinks from my mouth will become like me; I myself shall become that person, and the mysteries will be revealed to him."

109 Jesus said,

> The Kingdom is like a man who had a treasure hidden in his field but did not know it. And [when] he died, he left it to his [son]. The son [did] not know [about it either]. He took over the field and sold it. The buyer went plowing, [discovered] the treasure, and began to lend money at interest to whomever he wished.

110 Jesus said, "Whoever has found the world and has become wealthy, let him renounce the world."

111 Jesus said, "The heavens and the earth will roll up in your presence, and whoever is living from the living one will not see death." Does not Jesus say, "Those who have found themselves, of them the world is not worthy"?

112 Jesus said, "Woe to the flesh that depends on the soul. Woe to the soul that depends on the flesh."

113 His disciples said to him, "When will the Kingdom come?"

"It will not come by watching for it. They will not say, 'Look, it is here!' or 'Look, it is there!' Rather, the Kingdom of the Father is spread out upon the earth, but people do not see it."

114 Simon Peter said to them, "Make Mary leave us, for females are not worthy of life."

Jesus said, "Look, I shall guide her to make her male, so that she

too may become a living spirit resembling you males. For every female who makes herself male will enter the Kingdom of Heaven."*

┬o┬o┬o┬

I am grateful to Random House and Polebridge Press, and especially
grateful to Professor Marvin Meyer, who has graciously granted permission to consult the translation he published, with Professor Stephen
Patterson, as the Scholars Version in *The Complete Gospels,* and extended
to me, as to many of our colleagues, the benefit of his expertise.

Those who wish further to investigate the Gospel of Thomas and
the meaning of particular sayings (including the enigmatic saying 114)
may find the following publications especially useful:

Marvin Meyer, *The Gospel of Thomas: The Hidden Sayings of Jesus* (San
Francisco, 1992)

Marvin Meyer, *Secret Gospels: Essays on Thomas and the Secret Gospel of
Mark* (Harrisburg, Pa., 2003)

Willis Barnstone and Marvin Meyer, *The Gnostic Bible* (Boston, 2003)

Andrew Harvey, Stevan Davies (trans.), *The Gospel of Thomas: Anno-
tated and Explained* (London, 2003)

Stephen J. Patterson, *The Gospel of Thomas and Jesus* (Sonoma, Calif.,
1993)

Gregory J. Riley, *Resurrection Reconsidered: Thomas and John in Controversy* (Minneapolis, 1995)

Risto Uro, ed., *Thomas at the Crossroads: Essays on the Gospel of Thomas*
(Edinburgh, 1998)

Richard Valantasis, *The Gospel of Thomas* (London, 1997)

—Elaine Pagels

---

*The words *female* and *male* are not to be taken literally (as if they referred to woman
and man) but rather as characterizing respectively what is human and what is divine. See M. Meyer, *The Gospel of Thomas* (San Francisco, 1992), note on saying 114.

INDEX

ABOUT THE AUTHOR

After receiving her doctorate from Harvard University in 1970, Elaine Pagels taught at Barnard College, where she chaired the Department of Religion, and Columbia University. She is currently Harrington Spear Paine Professor of Religion at Princeton University. Professor Pagels has participated with other scholars in editing several of the texts from Nag Hammadi and has written several other books, including *The Gnostic Gospels; Adam, Eve, and the Serpent; The Origin of Satan;* and *The Gnostic Paul: Gnostic Exegesis of the Pauline Letters. The Gnostic Gospels* won the National Book Critics Circle Award and the National Book Award in 1980. In 1981 she was awarded a MacArthur Prize Fellowship. She lives in Princeton, New Jersey.